A Watched Cup Never Cools

Lab Activities for Calculus and Precalculus

Ellen Kamischke

KEY CURRICULUM PRESS
Innovators in Mathematics Education

Editor	Crystal Mills
Editorial Assistant	Jeff Gammon
Production Editor	Jason Luz
Copyeditor	Paul Green
Mathematics Checker	Dudley Brooks
Teacher Reviewers	Debbie Preston, Beth Schlesinger, Dixie Trollinger
Production Manager	Diana Jean Parks
Interior Design	Ann Rothenbuhler
Cover Design	Susan Schneider
Cover Design Coordinator	Diana Krevsky
Production and Layout	James Sununu, First Track Productions
Illustrations	Ben Turner Graphics
Student Work	Naomi Beeman, Parker Eberhard, John Greer, Lance Horne, Maggie Hulce, Elyse Johnson-Wolf, Chris Landau, Ian McClure, Stephanie Teply, Lin Wang, Alysia Williams, Freddy Yarur, Jin-Young Yu
Publisher	Steven Rasmussen
Editorial Director	John Bergez

Limited Reproduction Permission

Key Curriculum Press
P.O. Box 2304
Berkeley, CA 94702
510-548-2304
editorial@keypress.com
http://www.keypress.com

Printed in the United States of America   10 9 8 7 6 5 4 3 2 1   02 01 00 99 98
ISBN 1-55953-318-8

About the Author

Ellen Kamischke teaches mathematics at the Interlochen Arts Academy in Interlochen, Michigan. After graduating from Michigan Technological University with a degree in mathematics, she received an MAT in Physics from Michigan State University. She is a co-author with her husband, Eric Kamischke, and Jerald Murdock of *Advanced Algebra Through Data Exploration: A Graphing Calculator Approach*.

As a teacher, Ellen enjoys finding ways to incorporate the arts in her teaching and making the learning of mathematics both challenging and exciting for her students. She is particularly interested in fractals and chaos, number theory, and the history of mathematics.

Ellen has been a presenter at numerous regional and national mathematics conferences on topics from writing in mathematics to algebra at all levels and calculus. She was a participant in the Graphing Calculators in the Secondary Curriculum Summer Program at Central Michigan University and has participated in several symposiums on fractals, chaos, and dynamical systems. She has also been a presenter at the Key Curriculum Summer Institutes on Beginning and Advanced Algebra with Graphing Calculators.

When she's not writing textbooks, teaching, or presenting at conferences, Ellen enjoys solving puzzles, cooking (especially for her students), modern dance, being a mom to her daughter, Rachel, and trying to balance all the aspects of a busy and rewarding life.

CONTENTS

LAB ACTIVITIES

WRITING ASSIGNMENTS

Note to Teachers

The lab activities and writing assignments in this book were developed over a number of years while I was teaching AP Calculus. Some of the investigations are appropriate for a precalculus course as well as a calculus course. Just which ones are used and how will depend on the course and your students' ability levels. A Topic Chart is included to help identify where each lab activity fits in the curriculum. In cases where more than one topic is noted, the investigation seeks to tie concepts together and enable students to see the connections between the various ideas.

Lab Activities

The lab activities in this book serve a variety of purposes. Some of these investigations are designed to enable students to discover a new method or concept. Others are real applications of concepts they have learned previously. Most of the lab activities are designed to be done in small groups, while a few work best for students working in pairs or as projects for individuals. These distinctions are noted in the Grouping Chart following these remarks.

I usually allow students an average of two weeks to complete an activity working outside of class. The activities take considerably less time if students work on them in class. I have generally required three or four investigations per semester for each group of students. In addition, some of the shorter investigations have been used as extra credit options or class investigations. A brief equipment list follows the charts at the end of this Note. In most cases there are several alternatives when equipment is needed, so a lack of equipment should not preclude doing the investigation.

Writing Assignments

You can use the writing assignments in a variety of ways. Some of these topics can be used as prompts for journal entries. Others are useful as topics for review papers before an exam, or they can be used as alternative assessments in themselves.

I generally introduce the paper and then give students lots of time, sometimes several weeks, to complete it. I usually assign three or four papers per semester, allowing students the opportunity to rewrite their papers as frequently as they desire. Since students hand them in at different times, depending on where they are on the continuum of rough draft to final version, I never have too many papers at once to read and mark. In addition to correct mathematical ideas, I look for spelling (especially of mathematical vocabulary), basic grammar, and organization of the writing. I have consulted with an English teacher occasionally when a student's writing is "unusual." Grading papers gets easier with practice. I never assign a grade on a rough draft; I only offer comments and suggestions for improvement. When both the student and I are satisfied or the final deadline has come, then I put a grade on the paper. By then I am generally quite familiar with the paper and the final grade is not difficult to assign.

On the Grouping Chart, the topics are identified as minor or major, depending on the length of the paper I expect. Minor papers can usually be done well in one page or less. Major papers often take three or four pages.

Student Lab Reports

You may want to copy the page entitled Student Instructions for Writing a Standard Lab Report, although you may want to modify these instructions to suit your own particular specifications. Reports for various activities may differ. Activities that are very structured should take the form of summarizing what is done and learned in each step. Expect students to write their answers in complete sentences. Encourage students to explain what was learned in the step and not just answer the questions. In more open-ended activities, students should include detailed accounts of their procedures, even for those attempts that were not successful. By describing and analyzing what went wrong, students gain additional insight into problem solving. Students should annotate all calculations and equation work. They are learning to write for an educated audience. They need not explain every detail, but they should use proper vocabulary and express the ideas clearly. You should be able to follow their thinking and calculations without having to fill in too many gaps.

Group Evaluation Form

The Group Evaluation form provides an excellent opportunity for you to get some feedback on how the groups are working. I use this as a confidential report from them to me. Students should feel free to vent frustrations with other group members or with the activity itself in this document. They should be encouraged to complete the evaluation thoughtfully. To provide this encouragement, I award points for turning in a thoughtful evaluation for each lab. Reading the evaluations from various group members gives a picture of just what went on as they pursued the activity. Sometimes students within the same group will have very different assessments of just how much effort each person put in. If there is a consensus that some individual is not pulling her or his weight, I often speak with each member individually to get a clearer picture of exactly what the problems are. Then it is time to have a chat with the whole group. Without pointing fingers at the individual, you can discuss the responsibilities of each member of the group and how to make a successful effort on the next project. You may also want to have that group check in more frequently and report on what each individual is doing. It is also entirely appropriate to adjust individual scores on a project based on the input from evaluations.

Summary

Incorporating lab activities and writing assignments into a course takes time. However, the gains in understanding and appreciation of the power and usefulness of mathematics are well worth the effort and time spent. I hope that you and your students will find these activities challenging and rewarding.

Ellen Kamischke

Topic Chart

	Functions	Data analysis	Limits	Derivatives	Graphical analysis	Optimization	Related rates	Volumes	Surface area	Integration theorems
Foundation Work	✓									
Lines and Circles and Limits, Oh My!			✓							
What Goes Down, Must Come Up . . .		✓		✓	✓					
Mystery Curve	✓	✓	✓	✓	✓					
More Ice Cream, Please				✓		✓				
Prism Pop				✓		✓				
How Many Licks?		✓		✓			✓			
Is There No Limit to These Labs?				✓	✓					
A River Runs Through It	✓							✓		
A Watched Cup Never Cools	✓	✓		✓						
Home in the Dome								✓		
H_2O in the S-K-Y									✓	
It Averages Out in the End	✓									✓
Square Pegs in Round Holes		✓								✓
As Easy As π				✓				✓		
Let the Games Begin!								✓	✓	
Focus on Food	✓							✓	✓	
Lights, Camera, Action!	✓	✓	✓	✓	✓	✓	✓	✓	✓	
The Cup	✓	✓		✓			✓	✓	✓	✓
Mathematics and Me										
A Function by Any Other Name	✓									
Take It to the Limit				✓						
A Moving Experience				✓		✓				
The Meaning of Mean				✓	✓					
The Same, Yet Different										✓
Heads or Tails, Disks or Shells								✓		
The Game's Afoot	✓			✓						
Story Time	✓			✓						
Why Do We Have to Learn This?										✓
What Was It All About Anyway?	✓	✓	✓	✓	✓	✓	✓	✓	✓	✓

Grouping Chart

	Individual	Pairs	Groups of 3 or 4	Groups of 3 to 6	One hour or less	Up to one week	More than one week	Minor paper	Major paper
Foundation Work		✓	✓			✓			
Lines and Circles and Limits, Oh My!			✓			✓	✓		
What Goes Down, Must Come Up . . .			✓				✓		
Mystery Curve	✓	✓				✓			
More Ice Cream, Please			✓			✓			
Prism Pop	✓		✓	✓	✓	✓	✓		
How Many Licks?	✓				✓				
Is There No Limit to These Labs?		✓	✓			✓			
A River Runs Through It			✓				✓		
A Watched Cup Never Cools			✓			✓			
Home in the Dome	✓	✓				✓			
H$_2$O in the S-K-Y			✓				✓		
It Averages Out in the End		✓	✓			✓			
Square Pegs in Round Holes			✓				✓		
As Easy As π	✓	✓			✓				
Let the Games Begin!			✓	✓			✓		
Focus on Food			✓	✓			✓		
Lights, Camera, Action!			✓				✓		
The Cup			✓				✓		
Mathematics and Me									✓
A Function by Any Other Name								✓	
Take It to the Limit								✓	
A Moving Experience								✓	
The Meaning of Mean								✓	
The Same, Yet Different									✓
Heads or Tails, Disks or Shells									✓
The Game's Afoot								✓	
Story Time									✓
Why Do We Have to Learn This?									✓
What Was It All About Anyway?									✓

Equipment List

EQUIPMENT NEEDED	LAB ACTIVITY
Graphing calculator	Almost all activities
Electronic data collection device, motion detector, super ball	What Goes Down, Must Come Up . . .
Scissors, protractor	More Ice Cream, Please
Tootsie Roll Pops, rulers	How Many Licks?
Thermometer or electronic data collection device with temperature probe	A Watched Cup Never Cools Focus on Food
Cups or mugs, microwave or other heat source	A Watched Cup Never Cools
Hexagon-based dome tent	Home in the Dome
Tape measure, measuring sticks	Square Pegs in Round Holes
A variety of pie pans, rulers	As Easy As π
Video camera and tape	Lights, Camera, Action!
Plastic wine or champagne glasses	The Cup

Alternatives to many of the items on the equipment list or sources where you can find them are listed in the individual investigation notes.

Student Instructions for Writing a Standard Lab Report

The formats of the lab activities in this book vary greatly. Some of them are rather "cookbook" in structure. In some activities you are given a set of steps with questions to answer as you complete each step. Other activities are less structured, and you will have to define your own procedures and techniques. Some lab activities can be completed in an hour or two. Others will take several weeks to complete. However, your lab report for each activity should follow the guidelines given below.

- **Statement of Objective:** For some projects you are given the objective. For others you will have to determine why you are doing the investigation and what the goals are. Make this section of the report concise and clear.

- **Procedure:** In some projects this section will constitute much of the report. Do not write just the answers to each part of the question. Rather, summarize all that you did to answer each question and write your explanation in complete sentences. Include any graphs and tables that you were asked to make. The report should stand on its own. The instructor should not have to look at a copy of the project page in order to understand what is happening. For the less structured activities, include a complete explanation of the steps you followed, including why you chose to do the lab in that fashion. If you make several attempts to solve a problem, include a summary of your alternate attempts as well.

- **Data:** In some cases data will be included with the procedures. In other cases you will need to include a separate section on data collection. Always label the units of your data. Report your original data, and, if any alterations are made (data points dropped, values changed), explain why the changes were made and list the new data.

- **Calculations:** In many cases your calculations will be included with the procedures. Be sure that calculations are clearly labeled and commented upon when they are not entirely self-explanatory. When doing numerical calculations, keep the appropriate number of significant digits in mind. For example, if you are measuring to the nearest 0.1 centimeter, do not report an answer with eight decimal places. In general, be reasonable. If you have any questions as to how many digits to report, ask.

- **Graphs:** Each graph should be titled and the axes labeled with units indicated. Use appropriate scales. Graphs may be hand-drawn or downloaded from a computer or calculator. Use whatever technology presents the material most clearly.

- **Conclusions:** In this final section, summarize your results. What new techniques did you develop? What relationships did you discover? Were there any significant sources of error? If so, can you suggest improvements on the procedure to reduce these errors? Always be aware of significant digits and the reasonableness of your answers. If you are using actual measurements, be very careful with units.

Group Evaluation

Lab Project Title: _____

Group Members:

(In the box following each name, rate the contribution of each member on a scale of 1 to 5, with 1 indicating a limited contribution and 5 indicating a strong contribution.)

Your name _____ ☐

Other group members:

_____ ☐

_____ ☐

_____ ☐

Please respond to all of the following questions. If you need more space, use the back of this page.

1. **Describe your contribution to the project.** Specifically, describe what you did to assist in the completion of the project questions.

2. **Choose one statement that best characterizes your contribution to the group effort and explain.**

   ☐ I did more than my share.   ☐ I did my share.   ☐ I did not do my share.

3. **Choose one statement that best characterizes the contribution of each member to the group effort and explain.**

   ☐ Each member of the group contributed equally to the completion of the project.

   ☐ Other member(s) of my group contributed more than a fair share to the completion of the project. (Include name(s) of the group member(s) in question.)

   ☐ Other member(s) of my group did not contribute a fair share to the completion of the project. (Include name(s) of the group member(s) in question.)

4. **Were there difficulties in scheduling times to meet?** Explain.

LAB ACTIVITIES

LAB ACTIVITY *1*

Foundation Work

The objective of this activity is for you to review families of functions and transformations. You will be reviewing what you have learned in previous courses and extending your understanding of function families.

Equipment Needed

- Graphing calculator

PART 1

In the first part of this activity, you will explore the effects of multiplying or adding a constant to a function or its argument.

a. Choose several basic functions $f(x)$ to study. Compare the graphs of $y = f(ax)$ and $y = af(x)$ with the graph of $y = f(x)$. What effect does the number a have on the graph? Make a general statement about the relationships of the graphs of $y = f(ax)$ and $y = af(x)$ to the graph of $y = f(x)$.

b. Return to your basic functions and compare the graphs of $f(x + a)$ and $f(x) + a$ to the graph of $f(x)$. Make a general statement about the relationships of the graphs of $f(x + a)$ and $f(x) + a$ to the graph of $y = f(x)$.

PART 2

Define a function $f(x)$ for which the graph has the following features: at least one vertical asymptote, more than one x-intercept, a y-intercept, a horizontal asymptote. The graph should not be symmetric to the y-axis.

a. Graph your function and completely describe it.
b. Graph $|f(x)|$. How does the absolute value function affect the graph?
c. Repeat 2a and 2b for the function $f(x) = x^3 - 5x + 2$ to verify your conclusions.
d. Graph $f(|x|)$ and discuss the relationship of this graph to the graph of $f(x)$.
e. Repeat 2d using the function $f(x) = x^3 - 5x + 2$ to verify your conclusions.

f. In the figure at right, the graph of $y = g(x)$ is given. Copy this graph and on it sketch the graph of $|g(x)|$ on the same axes. Sketch the graph of $g(|x|)$ in another color. Write a justification for your sketches.

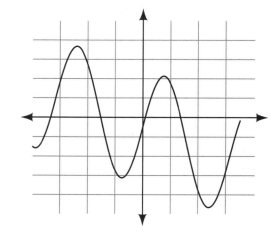

PART 3

In this part of the activity, you will explore the effect of the coefficient of the x-term in the parabolic equation $y = 3x^2 + bx - 2$.

a. First consider positive values of b. Describe how changing the b-value affects the shape of the parabola. Justify your answer.

b. Now consider negative values of b. Describe the effect that a negative b-value has on the graph of the parabola.

c. Combine your answers from 3a and 3b to make a general statement about the effect of the coefficient of the x-term in the parabola $y = 3x^2 + bx - 2$. Consider the location of the vertex as the value of b changes.

d. Write an equation for another parabola. Change the value of the linear coefficient. Does your hypothesis from 3c still apply? If not, modify it so that it does.

PART 4

Consider the quadratic polynomial $kx^2 + (k + 1)x - (k + 2)$, where k is a constant.

a. Graph the parabolas where $k = 1$, 2, 3, and 4. Compare the vertices and general shapes of these parabolas. What happens as k increases? Justify your answer.

b. Notice that all of these parabolas cross the x-axis at two points. Let s_k be the larger of the two solutions of $kx^2 + (k + 1)x - (k + 2) = 0$. Using your calculator, determine the values of s_1, s_2, s_3, and s_4.

c. Predict the behavior of s_k as k gets very large. Provide some support for your hypothesis.

TEACHER NOTES 1
Foundation Work

Prerequisite Knowledge

- Families of functions
- Function transformations

Equipment Needed

- Graphing calculator

The objective of this activity is for students to review families of functions and transformations. It also gives students a good chance to become more familiar with their graphing calculators. In this activity, students investigate parabolas having studied these graphs thoroughly in earlier courses. This investigation works well for groups of three or four students, though it can also be done in pairs. It generally takes students between one and three hours to complete this activity. It is an excellent idea to start this activity in class. Groups may need help in choosing basic functions for Part 1, and so you may want to see that they complete Part 1 and begin Part 2 before continuing on their own. Parts 3 and 4 involve a slightly different look at quadratics. The questions should provide students with additional insights and also introduce them to the concept of a limit.

Comments and Answers

Part 1

Good choices of functions to investigate include $y = \sin x$ or other trigonometric functions, $y = [x]$, $y = \ln x$, or $y = e^x$. Functions such as $y = x^2$ or $y = |x|$ do not show the difference between the two types of stretches nearly as clearly.

a. The graph of $y = af(x)$ is a vertical stretch of the graph of $y = f(x)$. The graph of $y = f(ax)$ is a horizontal stretch.

b. The graph of $y = f(x + a)$ is a horizontal shift of the graph of $y = f(x)$, while the graph of $y = f(x) + a$ is a vertical shift.

Part 2

The equations created will probably be rational functions. Piecewise functions are perhaps the easiest to create, but students should be encouraged to try to meet all the criteria with only one equation.

a. Students should list all of the features of the graph. Encourage them to use the proper vocabulary.

b and c. All portions of the graph for which $y = f(x) < 0$ will be reflected across the x-axis.

d and e. The portion of $f(x)$ for $x < 0$ will no longer appear. Instead, the portion of the graph for which $x > 0$ will be reflected across the y-axis and the graph will now be symmetric to the y-axis. Graphing $f(|x|)$ eliminates half of the original graph, replacing it with a reflection of the other half. Graphing $|f(x)|$ simply reflects each point below the x-axis to a point above it.

f. The graph pictured is the function $y = \frac{\pi}{1.05} \sin(2x) - \frac{\pi^2}{e^3}x - 0.5$. Don't expect students to discover this function. The intent of the question is for students to draw the requested functions by looking at the graph.

Graph of $|g(x)|$

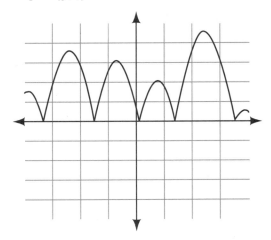

Graph of $g(|x|)$

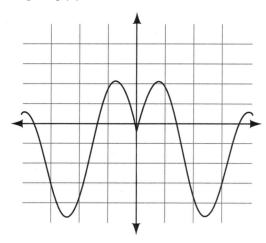

Part 3

a. As the value of b increases, the vertex of the parabola moves down and to the left. The justification can be a series of graphs for various values of b or an algebraic analysis.

b. As the value of b decreases, the vertex moves down and to the right. The justification can be a series of graphs for various values of b or an algebraic analysis.

c. The value of b affects the location of the vertex. As b increases in the positive direction, the vertex moves left and down. As b decreases in a negative direction, the vertex moves right and down. The vertices of this family of parabolas follow the parabola defined by the equation $y = -3x^2 - 2$. Students may not find the equation of this parabola, but they should note that the vertices appear to all lie on some parabola. In terms of b, the coordinates of the vertex are $\left(\frac{-b}{6}, \frac{-b^2}{12} - 2\right)$.

d. Students' answers for this may vary depending on the parabolas they investigate. In the most general case, they should find that the value of b affects the location of the vertex. For a parabola $y = ax^2 + bx + c$, the vertex will lie at the point $\left(\frac{-b}{2a}, \frac{-b^2}{4a} + c\right)$. All parabolas in the family will have vertices along the parabola $y = -ax^2 + c$.

Part 4

a. As the value of k increases, the vertices move down and to the right. The parabolas also become narrower due to the increasing quadratic coefficient. The justification can be a series of graphs for various values of k or an algebraic analysis.

b. The roots may be found using the quadratic formula, a root finder on the calculator, the calculator's solver routine, or approximations by tracing on the calculator. $s_1 = 1$, $s_2 = 0.8508$, $s_3 = 0.7863$, $s_4 = 0.75$

c. As k increases, s_k decreases. The limit is actually $\frac{-1 + \sqrt{5}}{2}$, the reciprocal of the golden ratio, $\frac{1 + \sqrt{5}}{2}$. (The smaller of the two solutions approaches the opposite of the golden ratio.) Students will probably only approximate s_k as 0.618. The roots can be found using the quadratic formula and then, when students try very large values of k, the values of the roots should approach this limit. This question is leading students toward the concept of a limit. Depending on the sophistication of the students, they may be ready to accept an intuitive argument for the actual value of the limit.

LAB ACTIVITY 2

Lines and Circles and Limits, Oh My!

Some limits are easy to predict, either algebraically or graphically. Others may arise from geometric situations and seem perfectly intuitive. However, some geometric situations create limits that are not intuitively obvious. In this activity you will look at some such situations. In each case, use as many tools as you have to explore: create algebraic expressions to model the situation, use your knowledge of geometry, try drawing it by hand. When you are convinced that you have found the correct limit, write up your conclusions, including all of your work and reasoning. Be thorough. Prove your answer.

Equipment Needed

- Graphing calculators (optional)
- Dynamic geometry software (optional)

PART 1

A circle of radius r, with $r < 1$, is centered at the origin. It is intersected by the circle with radius 1 centered at $(1, 0)$. A line is drawn through the point $(0, r)$ and the point of intersection of the two circles as shown. The function $f(r)$ defines the x-intercept of this line. What is the limit of $f(r)$ as r approaches 0?

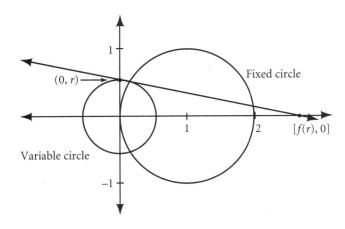

PART 2

Using the same two circles as defined in Part 1, draw a line tangent to the smaller circle at the point where the two circles intersect. The coordinate where this line intersects the *x*-axis is a function, $g(r)$, of the radius of the smaller circle. What is the limit of $g(r)$ as r approaches 0?

PART 3

Consider the ellipse $\frac{x^2}{a^2} + \frac{y^2}{b^2} = 1$. Draw a line tangent to the ellipse in the first quadrant at the point (c, d). Then draw a line perpendicular to this tangent through (c, d). The function, $h(c)$, defines the *y*-intercept of this perpendicular line. What is the limit of this function as *c* approaches 0? (Note: The slope of a tangent to an ellipse at any point (x, y) on the ellipse is given by $\frac{-b^2 x}{a^2 y}$.)

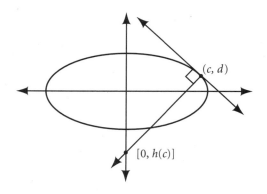

TEACHER NOTES 2
Lines and Circles and Limits, Oh My!

Prerequisite Knowledge

- Equations for circles, ellipses
- Equation of a line
- Skills in solving limits algebraically

Equipment Needed

- Graphing calculators (optional)
- Dynamic geometry software (optional)

The objective for this activity is for students to investigate some limits that are not intuitively obvious. Many tools can be used to help them. Some may wish to model the situation using Geometer's Sketchpad or a graphing calculator. Others may elect a purely algebraic approach. However, they should realize that numerical evidence for a limit is not a proof. For Part 1, the proof is algebraic. For Part 2, there is a simple geometric proof. For Part 3, again the proof is algebraic. Once students decide on a method of attack, this investigation proceeds quickly. This activity works well with groups of three or four students. Plan on at least a week outside of class to complete the entire investigation. If class time is used for the first part of the activity, the total time will be greatly reduced.

Comments and Answers

Part 1

Intuition seems to lead students to believe this limit is infinity. However, careful construction or numerical investigation leads to the surprising conclusion that the limit is 4, which is quite different from infinity.

The algebraic proof is outlined below.

The equations of the circles:

$$x^2 + y^2 = r^2 \qquad (x-1)^2 + y^2 = 1$$

The point of intersection:

$$\left(\frac{r^2}{2}, \frac{r}{2}\sqrt{4-r^2} \right)$$

The equation of the line:

$$y = \left(\frac{-2 + \sqrt{4 - r^2}}{r} \right) x + r$$

The x-intercept:

$$f(r) = \frac{-r^2}{-2 + \sqrt{4 - r^2}}$$

Rationalize the denominator and $f(r)$ becomes $2 + \sqrt{4 - r^2}$. Thus the limit of $f(r)$ as r approaches 0 is 4.

A geometric approach:

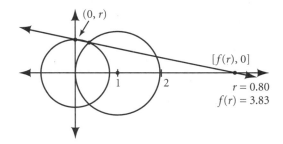

$r = 0.80$
$f(r) = 3.83$

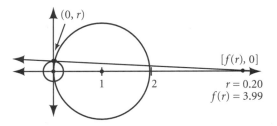

$r = 0.20$
$f(r) = 3.99$

To create the drawings shown above using The Geometer's Sketchpad, start by establishing a coordinate plane. Next construct the fixed circle. Then construct a point on the y-axis and, using the origin and the newly constructed point, construct a second circle. Construct the point of intersection of the two circles. Construct a line through the y-intercept of the variable circle and the point of intersection of the two circles. Construct the point of intersection of this line and the x-axis. Measure the coordinates of this point. Now vary the radius of the smaller circle and watch what happens to the value of the *x*-intercept.

Part 2

Once students have figured out the proof for Part 1, they will often just jump in to do an algebraic proof of Part 2 as well. They usually no longer trust their intuition and are not too surprised to find that the limit here is 2. A simple geometric proof is as follows: The tangent to the small circle will be perpendicular to the radius of this circle at the point of tangency. This means that the triangle formed by this radius, the diameter of the large circle, and the segment from the intersection point to the axis is a right triangle. The right angle is also an inscribed angle in the larger circle; thus, it cuts off a 180° arc and passes through the endpoints of the diameter.

To create this sketch using The Geometer's Sketchpad, begin by constructing the same two circles as in Part 1. Then construct the intersection point of the two circles. In order to construct the tangent to the variable circle at the point of intersection, first construct a line through the origin and the intersection point. Then construct a line perpendicular to this line at the point of intersection of the two circles. Locate the *x*-intercept of this line in the same fashion as in Part 1.

Part 3

Again, finding the limit in Part 3 is not intuitive. However, the mathematics of the proof are quite simple once the slope is known. The limit for this problem is $\frac{b^2 - a^2}{b}$.

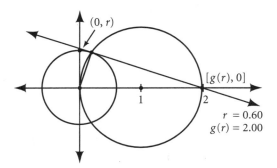

$r = 0.60$
$g(r) = 2.00$

LAB ACTIVITY 3

What Goes Down, Must Come Up . . .

In this activity you will investigate the relationships between position, velocity, and acceleration by numerically estimating derivatives based on data that you collect.

Equipment Needed

- Electronic data-collection device (CBL or equivalent)
- Motion detector
- Ball with at least a 50% rebound ratio per bounce
- Graphing calculator

PART 1
Collecting the data

a. Enter the program DROP into the calculator.
b. Connect the electronic data-collection device to the calculator using the link cable and the I/O ports located at the bottom edge of each unit.
c. Connect the motion detector to the SONIC port located at the left side of the electronic data-collection device. Make sure all connections are plugged in firmly.
d. Make sure the motion detector is fixed, level, and facing a hard, level surface.
e. Practice dropping the ball so that it bounces directly beneath the motion sensor. Hold the detector about 1 meter off the floor. Start the ball about 0.5 meters below the sensor.
f. Turn on the electronic data-collection device unit and the graphing calculator.
g. Run the program. Drop the ball after you hear the motion sensor start to make a "clicking" noise.

h. Look at the graph of your data. You need at least
two complete bounces of data. Three bounces are
better. Repeat the experiment until you have a good
set of data. The graph at the right shows a "good"
data sample. Notice that the data show the distance
between the sensor and the ball, not the height of
the ball. You will need to modify your data to show
the height above the floor.

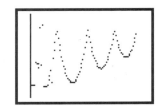

The DROP program consists of ten commands which are listed below. Notice that there
are two commands on each line. For the TI-85, you will need to use the second program
listing. It is not important that you know what each command does, but the explanation is
given for those who want to understand how the program works.

```
PROGRAM:DROP   --   82/83/86
{1,0}→L₁:Send(L₁)                              Reset, clear all probes
{1,11,2}→L₁:Send(L₁)                           Set sonic probe, measure in meters
{3,.02,99,0,0,0,0,0,1}→L₁:Send(L₁)            Read distance every 0.02 sec, make
                                               99 readings, remove noise from data

Get(L₂):Get(L₁)                                Get distance data, then time data
Plot1(Scatter,L₁,L₂,.):ZoomStat               Plot the data


PROGRAM:DROP   --   85
{1,0}→L₁:Outpt("CBLSEND",L₁)
{1,11,2}→L₁:Outpt("CBLSEND",L₁)
{3,.02,99,0,0,0,0,0,1}→L₁
Outpt("CBLSEND",L₁)
Input "CBLGET",L₂
Input "CBLGET",L₁
0→xMin:max(L₁)→xMax
0→yMin:max(L₂)*1.4→yMax
Scatter L₁,L₂
```

PART 2

Determining an approximate instantaneous velocity graph

You do not need to find an equation. Analyze the data only.

    a. Reproduce a paper copy of your data and graph.

    b. Explain how you generated velocity-time data from your distance-time data.

    c. Create a graph showing the velocity of the ball during its bounces. This will probably be a graph made up of points, rather than a smooth or connected curve.

    d. How can you explain the velocity graph? What is the velocity when the ball strikes the floor? How is this velocity shown in your graph?

PART 3

Determining an approximate acceleration graph

    a. Look at your velocity graph. How can you determine the acceleration of the ball from this graph?

    b. Create a graph of the acceleration of the ball. Explain the appearance of your graph.

PART 4

Extending and working backwards

    a. Go to the library or another reference source and find the value for the acceleration due to gravity on some other planet or moon of a planet.

    b. Using this information, construct an acceleration graph, a velocity graph, and a position graph for your ball assuming the experiment in Part 1 was performed in this alien location.

    c. Explain how you created these graphs and state any assumptions you made in doing so.

TEACHER NOTES 3
What Goes Down, Must Come Up . . .

Prerequisite Knowledge

- Average velocity as a numeric derivative of position
- Average acceleration as a numeric derivative of velocity
- Derivative as slope of a tangent to a curve
- Differentiability of a curve

Equipment Needed

- Electronic data-collection device (CBL or equivalent)
- Motion detector
- Ball with at least a 50% rebound ratio per bounce
- Graphing calculator

The objective of this investigation is for students to gain a better understanding of the relationships between position, velocity, and acceleration by numerically estimating derivatives based on data. This lab is appropriate for groups of three or four students. This investigation takes some time, up to two weeks if done outside of class. Collecting the data usually takes about a half an hour, depending on the floor and ball conditions. Parts 2 and 3 may take an hour or more each, though some students will complete them more quickly. Part 4 should take the longest; there is the most to consider and debate here. Students should plan on several hours for this final part and be prepared to thoroughly discuss their work with each other as this part is completed.

Comments and Answers

Part 1
Collecting the data

Before you have students collect the data, practice running the program and determine the best location for the collection. The floor beneath the electronic data-collection device should be smooth and firm. The type of ball used is also important. A large "super ball" usually works well. A firm basketball can also be used, but since the electronic data-collection device measures to the

top of the ball, when students adjust their data later they must not use the distance of the electronic data-collection device from the floor, but the distance from the electronic data-collection device to the top of the basketball when it is resting on the floor. Also, if the basketball is not firm enough, the bounces decay rather rapidly and it may be difficult to get enough good data. Students should try to get three good clear bounces of data. This may take several tries, so allow plenty of time for this part of the investigation. A sample data set is included for your use if students are unable to collect their own data.

If students use the sample data set provided, they will need to trim the first points off so that they work with just the data related to the bounces. Learning to interpret and work with real data is an important skill, thus the data was left untrimmed so that students can choose the data subset to use.

Part 2
Determining an approximate instantaneous velocity graph

Students should not try to fit an equation to the data. Rather, they should calculate the velocity based on the data by taking slopes of consecutive data points. They may do this using the list operations on their calculators. However, they must think carefully about the slopes between points at the end of the bounces. These slopes should promote a discussion among students of differentiability at the point of impact with the floor. Students must also decide what time value to associate with each calculated velocity. They should be encouraged to justify their decisions and to explain their reasoning as much as possible. The velocity graph should closely resemble a series of parallel line segments that become progressively shorter.

Part 3
Determining an approximate acceleration graph

Looking at the velocity graph, students have several choices of how to calculate accelerations. They may choose to determine the slopes between successive data points or they may calculate a least-squares fit for each linear section. The first method will probably yield a great variation in acceleration values, rather than the constant slope that they are expecting. This is because the velocities are average velocities, not instantaneous ones. Of course, the more original data points they have (the smaller the time interval in taking electronic data-collection device readings), the better the approximations of instantaneous velocities will be and the more constant the acceleration readings. If the students did not catch the problems of taking slopes between subsequent bounces, they will find some incredible accelerations if they continue to use slopes between each pair of points. Again, the discussions of differentiability, and now continuity, are important. Using a least-squares fit for the velocity data will generally yield good results. The slopes of each segment will be very close and often are quite close to the accepted value for the acceleration due to gravity.

Part 4
Extending and working backwards

This is a challenging section of the investigation. There are many assumptions that students must make and justify. Values for the acceleration due to gravity on other planets may be found in problems in their calculus book, almanacs, encyclopedias, astronomy books, and other reference materials. Information may also be found on the Internet. After finding a value for acceleration on another body, the acceleration graph is quite easy: a horizontal line. The velocity graph will be a series of parallel segments. However, the initial velocity is needed in order to place these lines on the graph. This is an important notion. The value for this initial velocity has no effect on the acceleration graph, yet it is needed to draw a velocity graph. This is the importance of "$+ C$" in an indefinite integral. Students should be able to justify their choice for an initial velocity. The time duration for each of these segments is another item of discussion. How will the time for the bounce on another planet compare to the time on earth? How will the time for each bounce compare to the time for the previous and subsequent bounces? Students should examine these questions for their real data and then make an assumption for their alien bounces. Look for good reasoning and strong arguments in their explanation of this graph. The position graph will likewise need to be justified. How high was the ball originally? This is another instance of needing to know or assume an initial value. How much does the height decay on each bounce? Is it the same as on earth? Why or why not? Students may wish to consult their physics teacher on some of these points. Class discussion of the issues is also helpful. A careful consideration of these points will deepen the students' understanding of the connections between position, velocity, and acceleration.

Sample Data Set for Lab 3, What Goes Down, Must Come Up . . .

Time (sec)	0.020	0.040	0.060	0.080	0.100	0.120	0.140	0.160	0.180
Distance (meter)	0.424	0.427	0.427	0.427	0.608	0.601	0.598	0.567	0.882

Time (sec)	0.200	0.220	0.240	0.260	0.280	0.300	0.320	0.340	0.360
Distance (meter)	0.585	0.903	0.421	0.416	0.418	0.417	0.430	0.465	0.505

Time (sec)	0.380	0.400	0.420	0.440	0.460	0.480	0.500	0.520	0.540
Distance (meter)	0.540	0.452	0.640	0.705	0.764	0.827	0.845	0.792	0.742

Time (sec)	0.560	0.580	0.600	0.620	0.640	0.660	0.680	0.700	0.720
Distance (meter)	0.696	0.654	0.616	0.580	0.549	0.523	0.500	0.481	0.467

Time (sec)	0.740	0.760	0.780	0.800	0.820	0.840	0.860	0.880	0.900
Distance (meter)	0.457	0.450	0.447	0.448	0.453	0.462	0.475	0.491	0.512

Time (sec)	0.920	0.940	0.960	0.980	1.00	1.02	1.04	1.06	1.08
Distance (meter)	0.536	0.564	0.597	0.633	0.675	0.719	0.767	0.819	0.855

Time (sec)	1.10	1.12	1.14	1.16	1.18	1.20	1.22	1.24	1.26
Distance (meter)	0.807	0.765	0.727	0.693	0.663	0.635	0.612	0.594	0.579

Time (sec)	1.28	1.30	1.32	1.34	1.36	1.38	1.40	1.42	1.44
Distance (meter)	0.569	0.562	0.559	0.560	0.565	0.573	0.586	0.603	0.623

Time (sec)	1.46	1.48	1.50	1.52	1.54	1.56	1.58	1.60	1.62
Distance (meter)	0.647	0.676	0.708	0.747	0.787	0.831	0.852	0.814	0.780

Time (sec)	1.64	1.66	1.68	1.70	1.72	1.74	1.76	1.78	1.80
Distance (meter)	0.749	0.723	0.698	0.682	0.665	0.654	0.647	0.644	0.645

Time (sec)	1.82	1.84	1.86	1.88	1.90	1.92	1.94	1.96	1.98
Distance (meter)	0.649	0.658	0.671	0.687	0.707	0.734	0.762	0.794	0.830

LAB ACTIVITY 4

Mystery Curve

In this activity you will explore the meaning of continuity, differentiability, and other analytic features of a curve. You will have to use the clues given below to find an equation for this mystery curve.

Equipment Needed

- Graphing calculator

The following five points lie on a function: $(1, 20)$, $(2, 4)$, $(5, 3)$, $(6, 2)$, $(10, 1)$. Find an equation that passes through these points and has these features:

a. There are three inflection points.
b. There is at least one local maximum.
c. There is at least one local minimum.
d. At least one critical point is not at a given point.
e. The curve is continuous and differentiable throughout.
f. The equation is not a single polynomial, but must be a piecewise defined function.

There are many possibilities that meet these criteria. Prove that your answer function does so.

$$y = \xi^{\alpha}_{3} \, {}^{\mu}\sqrt{N \langle \hat{x} | \breve{x} \rangle} \otimes \bigcap_{i=1}^{\infty} \succ \Phi \,|\, \sigma \neq \lambda^{47}$$

© 1999 Key Curriculum Press

TEACHER NOTES 4
Mystery Curve

Prerequisite Knowledge

- Critical points, continuity, differentiability, and their effect on the graph of a function as well as the associated equation

Equipment Needed

- Graphing calculator

This is a very open-ended investigation. The objective is to give students a chance to explore the meaning of continuity, differentiability, and other analytic features of curves. Because they are asked to find a curve that meets the given criteria, students must work through these meanings much more than they do in analyzing a given equation. Many possible approaches to the problem exist, and many possible answers also can be found. The final criterion that the equation not be a single polynomial causes some real problems for students. Without this restriction, the problem becomes much easier. One successful approach is to work with subsets of the points and fit curves to these subsets. Then create a connecting piece that maintains the continuity and differentiability of the curve. This lab can be completed by individual students or pairs of students. It is less effective for a larger group. Generally, a pair of students can complete the project in three to five hours.

Comments and Answers

One possible solution is shown below.

The equation for this curve is

$$y = \begin{cases} \dfrac{-49}{60}x^3 + \dfrac{209}{20}x^2 - \dfrac{1249}{30}x + 52 & x \le 6 \\[2ex] \dfrac{-301}{1440}x^3 + \dfrac{254}{45}x^2 - \dfrac{5951}{120}x + \dfrac{283}{2} & x > 6 \end{cases}$$

Find the first equation of the piecewise function by using the first four points in a cubic regression on the calculator. Evaluate the first derivative at the point (6, 2). Next, choose the points (6, 2), (10, 1), and an arbitrarily chosen point (12, −2) in the general cubic equation $ax^3 + bx^2 + cx + d = y$ to generate a system of three equations with four unknowns. Use the derivative of the general cubic equation, $3ax^2 + 2bx + c = y'$, at the point (6, 2), substituting y' with the value of the derivative found earlier. If you solve this system on a calculator, you obtain the second equation of the piecewise value.

LAB ACTIVITY 5

More Ice Cream, Please

Suppose you wanted to make an ice cream cone that would hold as much ice cream as possible. In this activity you will solve that problem.

PART 1

Cut a wedge from a circle and remove it. Form the remaining piece of the circle into a cone. Find the angle of wedge that produces the cone with the greatest volume.

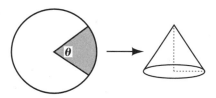

PART 2

Make a second cone from the removed wedge. Find a formula for the volume of this second cone in terms of θ, the angle of the wedge.

PART 3

Find the wedge angle that produces the maximum total volume of the two cones.

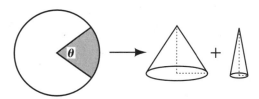

PART 4

Construct the actual cones for your answers in Parts 1 and 3. Consider carefully what size circle to start with. It may be difficult to construct the cones if your circle is either too small or too large for you to work with easily.

TEACHER NOTES 5
More Ice Cream, Please

Prerequisite Knowledge

- Formula for the volume of a cone
- How to find a maximum and verify it

Equipment Needed

- Paper
- Scissors
- Graphing calculator

The objective of this investigation is for students to model a situation and then optimize it. Also, it gives them the opportunity to incorporate their earlier geometry knowledge in a more complex situation. In addition, they should discover the value of the graphical and numerical approaches to derivatives as well as the symbolic approaches. This lab usually takes students between four and six hours to complete as a group. To shorten the time required, have students cut out circles in class and remove wedges. Then have them make these pieces into cones. Briefly discuss a strategy for finding a formula for the volume of the cone and how it might relate to the angle of the wedge. If the entire lab is done outside of class, allow two or three days for the first part, one day for the second and third, and one day for the fourth, or about one week total.

Comments and Answers

Part 1

The maximum volume is obtained when a 66.06° (1.153 radian) wedge is removed. In solving this problem students first must determine that the radius of the original circle is irrelevant. Usually they will then choose a convenient value for the radius and proceed. If a radius of 1 is chosen, then the volume of the cone will be

$$V = \frac{1}{3}\pi\left(1 - \frac{\theta}{2\pi}\right)^2 \sqrt{\left(1 - \left(1 - \frac{\theta}{2\pi}\right)^2\right)}$$

Taking the derivative of this equation is a formidable task. Some students will find this derivative by hand, but many will use a graphing calculator to graph the numerical derivative. When graphed, the derivative shows a clear root at 1.153 radians. They may also use a built-in maximum finder on a calculator. If so, they should provide some support for this value using calculus.

Part 2

The volume of the second cone is given by

$$V = \frac{1}{3}\pi\left(\frac{\theta}{2\pi}\right)^2 \sqrt{\left(1 - \left(\frac{\theta}{2\pi}\right)^2\right)}$$

Once students have found the equation for Part 1, this second equation usually presents little challenge.

Part 3

When the volumes are summed, a graph of the final volume equation appears to be a rather broad, flat-topped hill. If students investigate the graph more carefully, they will discover that the graph is actually concave up in the center and that there is a relative minimum there. Graphing the derivative of this volume equation gives a curve that may look cubic in nature. If students do not look carefully at this curve, they will not see that this equation actually has three roots. They may think there is only one root in the very center at $x = \pi$. However, this is a relative minimum and the maxima lie at the values $x = 2.036$ and $x = 4.247$ radians, or 116.65° and 243.35°.

Part 4

The only difficulties in this portion of the lab come from trying to make the cones either too small or too large. A good size is to start with a circle with a 10-centimeter radius, though nice cones can be made from many other sizes depending on the dexterity of the students and the materials used.

LAB ACTIVITY 6

Prism Pop

Why are pop cans the shape they are? What would happen if you changed to prism-shaped cans instead of cylinders? What would be the most cost-effective shape for a can of Prism Pop? Your team has been given the assignment of submitting a packaging plan for a new product. Prism Pop is to be sold in hexagonally based cans, each holding 355 milliliters of pop. The management prefers plans that lower the cost. The material for the sides costs 0.01 cents per square centimeter. The material for the bottom costs 0.03 cents per square centimeter. The material for the top costs 0.02 cents per square centimeter.

You also need to consider the cost of packaging and shipping in your plan. Consider carefully how many cans should be packed together and in what size and shape of containers. Assume that since you are a new company, you will rent trucks to ship the pop. Contact a truck rental company to find out the capacity and weight limits for various trucks. The cans will be sent from the plant in your town to distribution centers in two other towns that are each at least 1000 miles away. Assume that equal numbers of cans will be sent to each place. The exact numbers to be shipped are not known, but will be large. In other words, you will be able to fill any truck that you rent. You might want to consider calculating the cost per 500 or 1000 cans when deciding on what type of truck to rent.

You must submit a six-pack or other appropriate configuration of simulated cans and a sample shipping container. You must justify your design. Include details of shipping and the cost of your total plan. Convince the management that yours is the best strategy.

TEACHER NOTES 6
Prism Pop

Prerequisite Knowledge

- Formulas for volume of a prism and area of a hexagon
- How to find the maximum value of a function and verify it

Equipment Needed

- Graphing calculator
- Materials for building models of cans (these may include paper, cardboard, posterboard, tape, and glue)

The objective of this investigation is to give students a practical experience in optimization. The actual calculations may be quite simple. However, if students decide to include extra air space in the can to avoid "explosions" or decide to create a domed base as is found in real soda cans, the problem becomes more difficult. In the past, my students have contacted local bottling companies or national offices of large soft drink companies to ask questions about why certain design features are there and just how much air space to leave. This can be a fairly long-term project, taking up to two or three weeks outside of class if done well. The time needed for the investigation can be shortened if you leave out the packaging and shipping component and just focus on the can design. In fact, the first portion can be done in less than an hour and used as an assessment item when studying optimization.

When determining the shipping information, encourage students to experiment with different packing arrangements. Perhaps a standard six- or eight-pack is not the optimal shape. Also, change the plant location to your town and the distribution centers to two distant locations. When students investigate the weight of their shipments they should be reminded to include the weight of the packing materials along with the weight of the cans and soda. The number of cans is not specified. Students can assume they will have enough cans to fill any size truck. Figuring the cost per 1000 cans or a similar measure should help them decide how to ship them.

Rather than a standard lab report, an interesting twist is to have each group make a presentation of their plan and sample cans. You are the management of the company and will choose the best plan. They must try to convince you that their design is the most cost-effective and marketable. You might wish to have another teacher or adult also listen to the presentations and be part of the management team making the decision.

LAB ACTIVITY 7

How Many Licks?

In this activity you will determine the rate of change of volume
of a Tootsie® Roll Pop (TRP) as you consume it.

Equipment Needed

- Tootsie Roll Pop
- Graphing calculator

PART 1

Step 1 Determine the initial radius of the TRP.
(Assume it is a perfect sphere.)

Step 2 Place it in your mouth and carefully suck for
30 seconds.

Step 3 Measure the radius and record.

Step 4 Repeat steps 2 and 3 as many times as possible.

PART 2

From your data, determine the rate of change of the radius of the TRP for your mouth
power. This may or may not be a constant rate. If it is not constant, model it with some
function of time.

PART 3

Using your answer from Part 2, calculate how fast the volume is decreasing when the
radius is three-fourths its original value.

In your lab report include a description of your procedure, including how you
measured the radius and any difficulties you had. Include your data and calculations.
A well-known calculus text states that when sucked a TRP gives up volume at a rate of
0.08 milliliters per minute. Based on your experiment, comment on the reasonableness
of this value.

NOTES 7
ny Licks?

rerequisite Knowledge

- Formula for volume of a sphere
- Simple related rate problems
- How to find a rate of change from data
  (slope of a best-fit line or other technique)

Equipment Needed

- Tootsie Roll Pop for each student
- Graphing calculator

The objective of this investigation is to find a rate of change using real world imperfect data, showing how calculus can be applied even in these situations. This is a good lab for students to do independently over a weekend. It usually takes about an hour to completely finish the experiment and the write-up.

This investigation is fraught with sources of error. First of all, Tootsie Roll Pops are not perfect spheres. Secondly, measuring the radius may be a sticky job and doing it accurately, the same way each time, is a challenge. The most popular method is to wrap a string around the pop and then measure this circumference. Many students also use a ruler and just estimate the diameter.

Others have tried to use calipers or other precision instruments. The string method is probably the most reliable. Finally, sucking on the pop consistently is very difficult; tiring mouth muscles, hunger, the urge to bite—all serve to make consistent sucking almost impossible. Once the data are collected, the rate of change of the radius must be determined. Students should plot the radius as a function of time. For many students, this function will appear to be linear. Others may find that their data fit a nonlinear function. Once the value of dr/dt is determined at the appropriate moment, the value of dV/dt can be easily calculated. There is a wide variety of values for this experiment. Based on several years of experimentation, I have found that students who play a double reed instrument, such as a bassoon or oboe, usually have the greatest value for dV/dt. Among other musicians, pianists and string players usually have the smallest values.

LAB ACTIVITY 8

Is There No Limit to These Labs?

What happens when functions have limits that you can't seem to find using standard algebraic techniques? How can you determine those limits, if they exist? In this activity you will develop some new techniques to enable you to find these limits analytically.

PART 1

Consider the function $h(x) = \dfrac{\sin \frac{x}{3}}{e^{2x} - 1}$. You will investigate how this function behaves near $x = 0$.

a. Determine the limit as x approaches zero by zooming in graphically.

b. Determine the limit as x approaches zero by zooming in numerically. Make a table to record your investigations.

c. Based on your results in 1a and 1b, what do you think the limit is?

d. Find the linear approximations for the numerator and denominator functions at $x = 0$.

e. Replace the original numerator and denominator functions with these linearizations and find the limit.

f. Compare this limit to the answer from 1c. Explain.

g. Determine the derivatives of the numerator and denominator. What is the limit of the ratio of these expressions as x approaches zero?

h. Compare this limit to the answers from 1c and 1e. Explain.

PART 2

Repeat Part 1 for the function $h(x) = \dfrac{\ln (x + 1)^2}{x}$.

PART 3

Consider the function $h(x) = \dfrac{\ln (x + 1)^2}{x}$ again, this time as x becomes infinitely large.

a. Determine the limit both graphically and numerically as x grows infinitely large.

b. Graph the numerator and denominator functions separately. Compare their slopes as x grows infinitely large.

c. Determine the derivatives of the numerator and denominator functions. What is the limit of the ratio of these expressions?

d. Explain the connection between your answers to 3a and 3c.

PART 4

Describe some ways to get around the difficulty of trying to determine a limit of a rational function that takes an indeterminate form such as $\frac{0}{0}$ or $\frac{\infty}{\infty}$.

PART 5

Create functions of the form $h(x) = \frac{f(x)}{g(x)}$ that satisfy the given requirements.

   a. $\lim\limits_{x \to 0} f(x) = 0$, $\lim\limits_{x \to 0} g(x) = 0$, and $\lim\limits_{x \to 0} h(x) = 0$

   b. $\lim\limits_{x \to 0} f(x) = 0$, $\lim\limits_{x \to 0} g(x) = 0$, and $\lim\limits_{x \to 0} h(x) = 2$

   c. $\lim\limits_{x \to 0} f(x) = 0$, $\lim\limits_{x \to 0} g(x) = 0$, and $\lim\limits_{x \to 0} h(x) = \infty$

   d. $\lim\limits_{x \to 0} f(x) = \infty$, $\lim\limits_{x \to 0} g(x) = \infty$, and $\lim\limits_{x \to 0} h(x) = 0$

   e. $\lim\limits_{x \to 0} f(x) = \infty$, $\lim\limits_{x \to 0} g(x) = \infty$, and $\lim\limits_{x \to 0} h(x) = 2$

   f. $\lim\limits_{x \to 0} f(x) = \infty$, $\lim\limits_{x \to 0} g(x) = \infty$, and $\lim\limits_{x \to 0} h(x) = \infty$

PART 6

Consider the graphs of the functions $f(x)$ and $g(x)$ shown below.

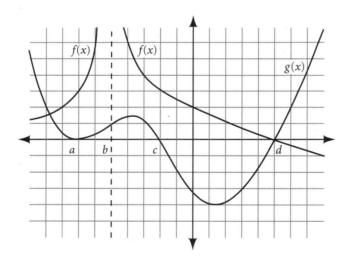

Suppose $h(x) = \frac{f(x)}{g(x)}$ and $k(x) = \frac{g(x)}{f(x)}$. Determine the following limits and explain how you found them. If it is not possible to find the limit, explain why not.

   a. $\lim\limits_{x \to a} h(x)$ b. $\lim\limits_{x \to d} h(x)$ c. $\lim\limits_{x \to \infty} h(x)$

   d. $\lim\limits_{x \to b} k(x)$ e. $\lim\limits_{x \to d} k(x)$ f. $\lim\limits_{x \to \infty} k(x)$

TEACHER NOTES 8
Is There No Limit to These Labs?

Prerequisite Knowledge

- How to find limits numerically, graphically, and symbolically
- Derivatives of polynomial, trigonometric, and exponential functions
- How to write a linear approximation to a curve at a given point

Equipment Needed

- Graphing calculator

The objective for this lab is to lead students to the discovery of L'Hôpital's Rule. They examine functions that approach $\frac{0}{0}$ as x approaches a specific value. By comparing the limits numerically and graphically, they determine a value for the limit. Then by replacing the numerator and denominator functions with linear approximations at the point in question, they find the limit of the ratio of these new functions and discover it to be the same value as before. In considering the case of $\frac{\infty}{\infty}$, students are asked to first determine the limit both numerically and graphically. Then they examine the slopes of the numerator and denominator functions as x becomes larger. The ratio of these slopes is the same as the value they found numerically and graphically. Students then apply these concepts to create new functions of the form $\frac{f(x)}{g(x)}$ that approach $\frac{0}{0}$ and $\frac{\infty}{\infty}$ but have actual limits of zero, 2, or infinity. The purpose of this part of the activity is to reinforce the fact that the forms $\frac{0}{0}$ and $\frac{\infty}{\infty}$ are indeed indeterminate and no assumptions can be made as to the actual limits without further investigation. In the final part of the lab students apply these concepts to functions known only graphically. To determine some of the limits requested, students must apply L'Hôpital's Rule by approximating slopes.

This investigation generally takes two full class periods or three to five days outside of class. It may be started with students doing Parts 1 and 2 in class and then completing the rest of the investigation outside of class.

Comments and Answers

Part 1

a. The graph appears to approach the value 0.166. Care must be taken not to zoom in too far as distortion will occur for extremely small values of x, usually within $1 \cdot 10^{-13}$ of zero. Depending on the calculator, the portion of the graph extremely near the y-axis may even disappear.

b. Numerical values also show the function approaching the value $1.1\overline{6}$. Again, if the x values are too close to zero, the function values may be distorted or show up as errors on the calculator.

c. The limits are the same both numerically and graphically.

d. Linear approximation for the numerator:
$y = \frac{1}{3}(x - 0) + 0$ or $y = \frac{1}{3}x$
Linear approximation for the denominator:
$y = 2(x - 0) + 0$ or $y = 2x$
Students should show details of this work.

e. $\lim\limits_{x \to 0} \dfrac{\frac{1}{3}x}{2x} = \lim\limits_{x \to 0} \dfrac{1}{6} = \dfrac{1}{6}$

f. It is the same value as found numerically and graphically.

g. $f'(x) = \frac{1}{3}\cos\frac{x}{3}, g'(x) = 2e^{2x}$
$\lim\limits_{x \to 0} \dfrac{\frac{1}{3}\cos\frac{x}{3}}{2e^{2x}} = \lim\limits_{x \to 0} \dfrac{\frac{1}{3}}{2} = \dfrac{1}{6}$
Students should show details of these derivatives and the limit calculation.

h. It is the same value. Since the numerator and denominator functions are each continuous and differentiable at $x = 0$, they may be approximated by their tangent lines. The limits along these approximations will be the same as the limits of the functions since they are equal at the point of tangency. Thus, it is reasonable to use the linear approximations in place of the actual numerator and denominator functions. Since the value of each function is zero at the x value in question, the linear approximations are each of the form $y = m(x - x_0)$. The ratio of these functions reduces to a ratio of the slopes, which are the values of the derivatives at $x = 0$. So, using the ratio of the derivatives is essentially the same as using the ratio of the linear approximations.

Part 2

Answers should be similar to those for Part 1. In this case the limit is 2. Be careful entering this function in a calculator. On some calculators you may need an extra set of parentheses to ensure that the correct quantity is being squared. In some cases $\ln(x + 1)^2$ may be interpreted as $(\ln(x + 1))^2$. Check to see what happens on the type of calculator your students use. You may wish to tell them to enter the function as $\ln((x + 1)^2)$.

Part 3

a. Graphically the curve appears to be asymptotic to the x-axis. Numerically the limit approaches zero.

b. The numerator function has a decreasing slope that seems to approach zero while the denominator has a constant slope of one.

c. $f'(x) = \dfrac{2}{x + 1}, g'(x) = 1$

$$\lim_{x \to \infty} \frac{\frac{2}{x + 1}}{1} = 0$$

d. They are the same value. As x becomes infinitely large, the numerator is growing very slowly. The denominator grows at a steady pace. So even though both are becoming infinite, the numerator becomes relatively insignificant in comparison to the denominator. Comparing the derivatives of the two functions lets us look at these rates of growth. Their ratio gives us the ratio of the actual values of the functions even when the values are both infinite.

Part 4

The limit may be determined numerically by evaluating the rational function for values closer and closer to the limit point. It may also be seen graphically by zooming in or out toward the limiting value. In addition, you may also consider the

ratio of the derivatives or slopes of the numerator and denominator functions instead of the original function. The limit of this ratio is the same as the limit of the original rational function.

Part 5

Many functions are possible. Following is one set of answers. Encourage students to work with combinations of simple functions in creating these.

a. $f(x) = \cos(x) - 1, g(x) = \sin(x)$

b. $f(x) = 2\sin(x), g(x) = x$

c. $f(x) = \sin(x), g(x) = x^3$

d. $f(x) = \dfrac{1}{x^2}, g(x) = \dfrac{1}{(\sin x)^4}$

e. $f(x) = \dfrac{2}{x^2}, g(x) = \dfrac{1}{(\sin x)^2}$

f. $f(x) = \dfrac{1}{x^4}, g(x) = \dfrac{1}{(\sin x)^2}$

Part 6

Students will need to approximate slopes of each of the two given functions. Distribute a copy of the graph for them to use in their calculations.

a. $\lim\limits_{x \to a} h(x) = \infty$. The numerator approaches 3 while the denominator approaches zero.

b. $\lim\limits_{x \to d} h(x) \approx -0.18$. Draw the tangents at $x = d$ and measure their slopes. The ratio is about -0.18, depending on how the slopes are measured.

c. $\lim\limits_{x \to \infty} h(x) \approx -0.1$. Draw tangents at the rightmost points on the graphs and measure the slopes. The ratio is about -0.1, depending on how the slopes are measured.

d. $\lim\limits_{x \to b} k(x) = 0$. The numerator approaches a finite value while the denominator becomes infinite. This causes the overall function to approach zero.

e. $\lim\limits_{x \to d} k(x) \approx -5.7$. Draw the tangents at $x = d$ and measure the slopes. The ratio is about -5.7, depending on how the slopes are measured.

f. $\lim\limits_{x \to \infty} k(x) \approx -10$. Draw tangents at the rightmost points on the graphs and measure the slopes. The ratio is about -10, depending on how the slopes are measured.

LAB ACTIVITY 9

A River Runs Through It

What happens when a toxic substance is dumped into a lake? How long does it take before all of this substance is eliminated? In this activity you will determine the volume of Green Lake and the amount of time to reduce the concentration of a pollutant by half its original value.

PART 1

Determine the volume (in gallons) of water of your assigned section of Green Lake. Then make a brief presentation of your results and describe the methods you used. Do not go into all of the excruciating details of your calculations, but describe your method well enough that others could repeat it. Be sure that your final answer is stated clearly and with the correct units (gallons).

PART 2

Combine your results with those of the other groups and calculate the total volume of the lake.

PART 3

Based on calculations made by previous calculus classes, water flows into the lake at approximately 1.5 million gallons per hour. Since the lake is not changing its level (not much, anyway, over the course of a year), the same amount of water must be leaving the lake. Suppose that some environmentally unconscious person dumps 5000 gallons of ammonia into the lake. Assume that it mixes throughout the lake uniformly. Determine the initial concentration of ammonia in the lake in parts per million. How long will it take to reduce that concentration to half its original value? Explain your reasoning and work in your written report. Include a written explanation and complete calculations for your volume portion of the project. (Note: This project may not actually involve any calculus. Nevertheless, you will be working with some of the same concepts, applying them to a real setting.)

TEACHER NOTES 9
A River Runs Through It

Prerequisite Knowledge

- How to read a topographic map
- Numeric and geometric methods of approximating area of a given region
- Calculations of exponential decay

Equipment Needed

- Topographic map of Green Lake or a lake in your area
- Graphing calculator

The objective of this lab is for students to extend their knowledge of area approximation methods to develop volume approximations. A map of a local lake may be substituted for the map of Green Lake. Fishing stores or conservation clubs often have maps showing depth intervals. Divide the lake into sections, one section per group. Post a copy of the map for all to see. Use a photocopier to make larger views of each section. Distribute these section maps to groups. The Green Lake map and sectional maps provided may be used for different numbers of groups since no section boundaries are drawn. Mark your group sections on the main map and then transfer these boundaries to the others. Groups of three or four students work well for this project. It usually takes about two weeks outside of class for students to complete the entire project. Most of this time will be spent on the first portion of the lab. Once the total volume is known, Part 3 can be completed quickly. One or two days should be sufficient for students to finish their calculations and add final touches to their reports. Encourage students to write up the lab as they go and not wait until the end.

Comments and Answers

Part 1

My students have been very creative in this problem. Some of their solution methods are described below.

a. Students covered each depth section of the group's portion of the map with small beads and then transferred the same beads to graph paper and counted the number of squares covered. This total was then converted to an area measurement and, by using the map scale, to an actual area. Students then used the average depth between the depth lines to convert this measure to a volume.

b. Students cut out each depth section of the group's portion of the map. Then they cut these sections into regular geometric shapes and measured them. They then used the average depth as in method a.

c. Students traced each depth section and then overlaid this tracing on graph paper. They divided the area into regular shapes (rectangles, triangles, and so on) and determined the area based on the graph paper scale. They then used the map scale and average depth as in method a.

d. Students scanned the map into the computer and wrote a computer routine to count the number of pixels in each section. Then they converted this number to an area measurement and found the average depth as in method a.

e. Students determined the area of the whole section by using regular standard shapes (rectangles, triangles, and so on). They multiplied this area by the average depth between the first two rings. This is the volume of the top layer. Then they cut away the outermost ring and determined the area of the remaining section. They multiplied this result by 10, the depth for this layer. Next they cut away the outermost ring, determined the area, and multiplied by 10. They repeated this process until the volumes of all layers were determined. Finally, they calculated the sum of the volumes of all of the layers.

There are many other variations on these ideas. Let the students be creative.

Presentations can be made many ways. They can be videotaped, written up on poster board, given orally, or put on a computer for all to read. Whatever method you choose, the information should be available to all. Learning how other groups tackled the problem is very interesting to students.

Part 3

The river that enters and leaves Green Lake is rather small, about 35 feet across at the mouth. It varies in depth, occasionally as deep as 8 feet, more often about 4 or 5 feet at the center. If you are using a different lake and do not have access to this information for your particular setting, either adjust the value of 1.5 million gallons per hour or use it as is. The amount of ammonia is actually quite small in comparison to the volume of this lake. Nevertheless, it is amazing to see just how long it takes the amount of pollutant to be reduced by half. A biology or ecology teacher may have data on flushing time for area lakes. This value is calculated a little differently, but the result is about the same as the one students will get by doing an exponential decay. For example, the volume of Green Lake, according to the latest calculations by my students, is about $2.06 \cdot 10^{10}$ gallons.

Since $1.5 \cdot 10^6$ gallons leaves every hour, this means that $\frac{1.5 \cdot 10^6}{2.06 \cdot 10^{10}} = 7.28 \cdot 10^{-5}$ or 0.00728% of the lake is changed each hour. The initial concentration of ammonia is $\frac{5000}{2.06 \cdot 10^{10}} = 2.43 \cdot 10^{-7}$ or 0.243 parts per million. To reduce this value by half means to reach a concentration of 0.1215 parts per million. Using the equation for exponential decay $0.1215 = 0.243 (1 - 7.28 \cdot 10^{-5})^x$, and solving for x gives the value of approximately 9521 hours or 397 days. This result is surprising to most students, but is actually very reasonable for a small lake. Larger lakes may take much longer to flush out a spill. The largest factor is the rate at which the lake water is refreshed by incoming streams and outgoing flow. Of course many assumptions have been made here that are not practical, such as the assumption that all the ammonia will mix uniformly throughout the lake and that none of it is lost through evaporation. These assumptions affect the results of the calculations, but not significantly.

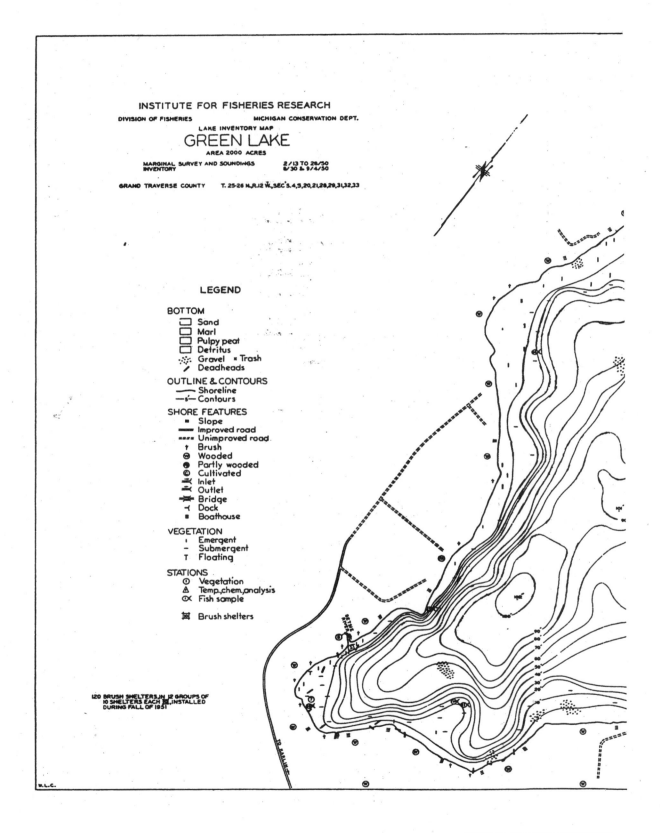

INSTITUTE FOR FISHERIES RESEARCH

DIVISION OF FISHERIES   MICHIGAN CONSERVATION DEPT.

LAKE INVENTORY MAP

GREEN LAKE

AREA 2000 ACRES

MARGINAL SURVEY AND SOUNDINGS   2/13 TO 28/50
INVENTORY   8/30 & 9/4/50

GRAND TRAVERSE COUNTY   T. 25-26 N,R,12 W, SEC S. 4,5,20,21,28,29,31,32,33

LEGEND

BOTTOM
▢ Sand
▢ Marl
▢ Pulpy peat
▢ Detritus
Gravel   ▪ Trash
/ Deadheads

OUTLINE & CONTOURS
— Shoreline
—s— Contours

SHORE FEATURES
▪ Slope
━ Improved road
▪▪▪▪ Unimproved road
↑ Brush
⊖ Wooded
◑ Partly wooded
◔ Cultivated
Inlet
Outlet
Bridge
Dock
Boathouse

VEGETATION
| Emergent
- Submergent
T Floating

STATIONS
⊙ Vegetation
△ Temp,chem,analysis
Ⓧ Fish sample

Ⅲ Brush shelters

120 BRUSH SHELTERS,IN 12 GROUPS OF
10 SHELTERS EACH ,INSTALLED
DURING FALL OF 1951

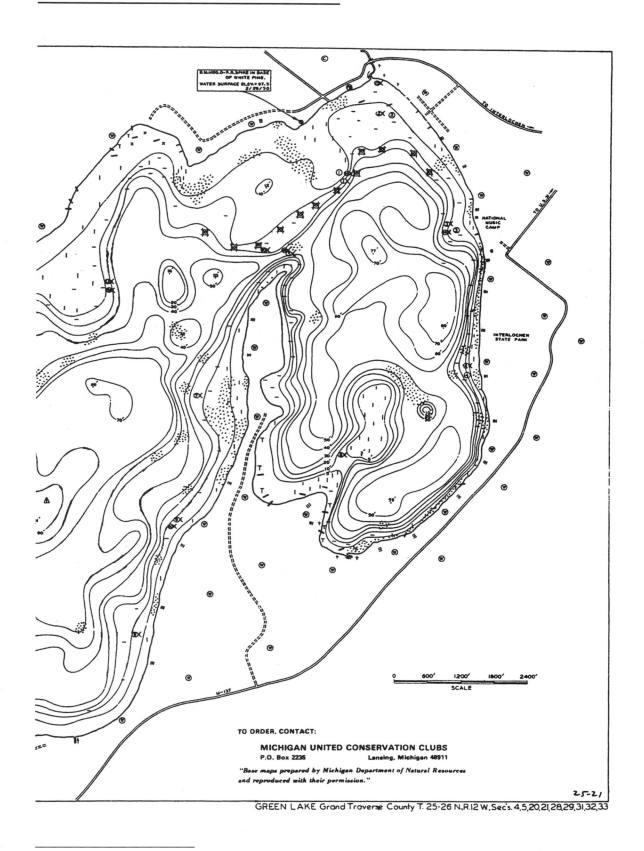

TO ORDER, CONTACT:

MICHIGAN UNITED CONSERVATION CLUBS
P.O. Box 2235   Lansing, Michigan 48911

*"Base maps prepared by Michigan Department of Natural Resources
and reproduced with their permission."*

25-21

GREEN LAKE Grand Traverse County T. 25-26 N, R.12 W, Sec's. 4,5,20,21,28,29,31,32,33

LAB ACTIVITY *10*

A Watched Cup Never Cools

When you have a hot cup of coffee, how long does it take until the liquid in the cup reaches room temperature? You might be surprised by the answer to this question. In this activity you will discover the mathematical relationship that describes how a cup of hot water cools.

PART 1

Fill a cup or mug with water. Heat the water to near boiling, about two or three minutes in a microwave oven. Wait a minute or two for the cup to heat up as well. Record the room temperature. Record the temperature of the water over the next three or more hours as it cools. Be sure the thermometer or temperature probe is in the water, not touching the cup bottom or wall. Enter these data points (or a subset of them) into your calculator and graph them.

PART 2

Find an equation that best fits your data. Examine the residuals to help fine tune your equation.

PART 3

Determine the slope between every two data points. These slope values give the rate of cooling in degrees per unit time. How does it change? Graph this rate of cooling. Explain how you determined your graph. Describe any relationship you see between this graph and the graph of the original data.

PART 4

Alter the data by subtracting room temperature from each temperature measurement. Find the percent change in temperature per minute and graph this. Explain the appearance of the graph. Does this give you any additional insight?

Along with your original data and an explanation of your procedures, your report should include the following elements:

- a graph of the data;

- a graph of the residuals and an explanation of what they tell you;

- a graph of the cooling rate and an explanation of how you made it and how it relates to calculus;

- a graph of the percent change and what this tells you and how it relates to calculus.

The programs below, for several TI calculators, can be used to collect the data using an electronic data-collection device. It is not nearly as exciting to use the electronic data-collection device as it is to sit there for four hours watching a thermometer in a cup of hot water, but it is more convenient. Run the first program, COOL, to give instructions to the electronic data-collection device. Press the trigger button on the electronic data-collection device to start the data collection. If you incorrectly entered any of the information, simply run the program COOL again and enter the correct information. Now you may disconnect your calculator and let the electronic data-collection device work. When the electronic data-collection device reads DONE on the display, you should reconnect the calculator and run the program GETDATA. Note that the TI-86 version of COOL is the same as the TI-82 and TI-83 versions, but the GETDATA program is a little different.

```
PROGRAM:COOL  --  82/83/86
{1,0}→L₁:Send(L₁)                        Reset, clear all probes
{1,1,10}→L₁:Send(L₁)                     Set temp probe, measure in °C
Disp "INTERVAL BETWEEN"
Disp "READINGS (SECS)"
Prompt S                                 Read temp every S sec
Disp "TOTAL NUMBER OF"
Disp "DATA POINTS"
Prompt N                                 Collect N measurements
Disp "TOTAL TIME (HRS)"
Disp S*N/3600
Disp "PRESS TRIGGER TO"
Disp "START"
{3,S,N,1,0,0,0,0,1}→L₁:Send(L₁)
```

```
PROGRAM:GETDATA  --   82/83
Get(L₂):Get(L₁)                               Get temp data, then time data
Plot1(Scatter,L₁,L₂,.):ZoomStat              Plot data
```

```
PROGRAM:COOL  --  85
{1,0}→L1:Outpt("CBLSEND",L1)
{1,1,10}→L1:Outpt("CBLSEND",L1)
Disp "INTERVAL BETWEEN"
Disp "READINGS (SECS)"
Prompt S                                      Read temp every S sec
Disp "TOTAL NUMBER OF"
Disp "DATA POINTS"
Prompt N                                      Collect N measurements
Disp "TOTAL TIME (HRS)"
Disp S*N/3600
Disp "PRESS TRIGGER TO"
Disp "START"
{3,S,N,1,0,0,0,0,1}→L1
Outpt("CBLSEND",L1)
```

```
PROGRAM:GETDATA  --  85
Input "CBLGET",L2
Input "CBLGET",L1
0→xMin:max(L1)→xMax
0→yMin:max(L2)*1.4→yMax
Scatter L1,L2
```

```
PROGRAM:GETDATA  --  86
Get(L2):Get(L1)
Plot1(1,L1,L2,1):ZData
```

TEACHER NOTES 10
A Watched Cup Never Cools

Prerequisite Knowledge

- Exponential functions
- Data analysis skills (modeling data and using residuals to refine the model)
- Derivative as rate of change

Equipment Needed

- Mug or cup
- Water
- Heating source (burner, hot pot, coffee maker, microwave, etc.)
- Thermometer or electronic data-collection device with a temperature probe

Newton's law of cooling is a standard part of most calculus courses. However, it describes an ideal situation. In real life things don't always work that way. Other factors influence the situation and Newton's law is only a model, not necessarily what actually happens in every circumstance. In this lab students collect data from a cooling cup of water over a long time period. The time is long in order to collect enough data to see the asymptotic behavior of the curve and also to catch the rapid cooling at the beginning. Time intervals for data collection are not specified. Students should decide how often they want to collect the data. Generally they choose to read the thermometer every minute or two at the beginning and then spread the readings out as the temperature changes more slowly. If you are using an electronic data-collection device, the readings will probably be at regular intervals. Depending on the calculator used, you may want to take readings every two minutes, five minutes, or other time interval. Let students make this decision based on their own experiences with cooling cups of coffee or other hot liquid. In a precalculus setting you may wish to assign specific time intervals to different groups.

This lab can be used as an introduction to derivatives of exponential functions or after students are familiar with this topic. In Part 3 they graph an approximation of the derivative. Seeing the connection to the original equation helps make sense of the rule for the derivative. Ask students to find an equation for this derivative if you wish.

This lab generally takes four to six hours to complete after collecting the data. Data collection can be done during the school day with students taking turns during free hours, study halls, or lunch hours. If this is not possible, use the sample data provided.

Comments and Answers

Part 1

The data collected will show a rapid decrease in temperature at the beginning and then a slowing of this cooling as it approaches room temperature. Students will probably be surprised to find out that after three or even four hours, the water is still slightly above room temperature.

Part 2

The equation should be exponential. Have students show you their equation as they progress. If they try other types of functions, have them consider such questions as "Would your function have predicted the temperature before you collected the data?" If they have used $1/x$ as the parent function for their curve, they will note that it gives the starting temperature as infinite and the temperature before the starting time as negative. Another question to consider is "Does your function predict the temperature into the future?" If they have used a quadratic, it will predict an eventual rise in temperature. Other functions may predict that the temperature will eventually fall below freezing. Considering such ideas as these helps to eliminate all but an exponential function.

Beware of students trying to use the built-in exponential regression on their calculator. The built-in regression will fit an exponential curve to the data, but it will be a curve that is asymptotic to the x-axis and consequently a very poor fit. If students wish to use the built-in regressions, they must first alter their data as in Part 4, do the regression, and then modify the equation by adding the room temperature as a constant.

Residuals are an excellent tool to use to fine tune the equation. Residuals are the differences between the data points and the values on the theoretical curve. If a data point lies above the curve, the residual is positive. If it lies below, the residual is negative. The best scenario is to have an equal number of positive and negative residuals, and they should all be small in absolute value. In addition, if these values are plotted, they should show no pattern (for example, positive residuals for small values of x and negative residuals for large values of x). Any pattern, curved or linear, indicates that the function chosen does not completely or accurately describe the data.

Residuals showing a good fit.

Residuals showing a poor fit.

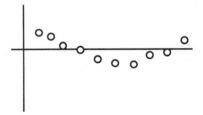

Typical residuals for a cooling experiment show a pattern when Newton's law of cooling is used, because there are other factors influencing the experiment. The temperature of the cup is not constant throughout; it is the same temperature as the water on its inner surface, and cooler on the outside. This loss of heat through the cup affects the cooling of the water itself. In addition, there are convection currents within the water and air currents that affect the cooling from the surface. Also, room temperature is apt to vary. Taken together, these factors cause the cooling water not to behave exactly as expected. The residual graph below is typical. Students can adjust their equations to improve the residuals, but the shape shown below will most likely remain.

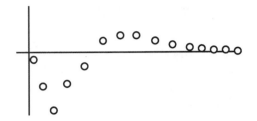

Part 3

This graph is the derivative of the data. The slopes start out large though negative, and then gradually move toward zero. Thus, the graph should also appear to be exponential. This time the graph is increasing, with the x-axis as an asymptote. If students try to fit an equation to this new data, they should find that the derivative of their original equation works fairly well.

Part 4

After the data are altered, it will be asymptotic to the x-axis. Students can find the percent change per minute in at least two ways. One way is to solve the equation $y_{n+1} = y_n(1 - r)^m$ where y_{n+1} and y_n are two successive data points and m is the number of minutes elapsed between data points. The value of r is the percent change in temperature each minute during this time period. Solving this equation for each pair of successive data points gives the percent change per minute throughout the experiment.

A less accurate method is to find the percent change between each two successive data points and then divide these values by the number of minutes in each time interval. These values will only be approximations for the percent change per minute, but if the data points are relatively close together, they will provide a reasonable approximation. Regardless of how it is calculated, the percent change per minute should be a fairly steady value. There will be variation during the first part of the experiment, due to initial warming of the cup and establishment of the system. There will also be variation during the last part of the experiment because of the sensitivity of the equipment, but over all, the value should not vary too much. This result verifies that the relationship is exponential.

Sample Cooling Data for Lab 10, A Watched Cup Never Cools

Room temperature was 21°C when this data was collected.

Time (sec)	0	180	360	540	720	900	1080	1260	1440
Temp (°C)	83.79	75.71	70.11	65.58	61.68	58.57	55.96	53.48	51.53

Time (sec)	1620	1800	1980	2160	2340	2520	2700	2880	3060
Temp (°C)	49.64	47.82	46.17	44.69	43.36	42.05	41	39.84	38.93

Time (sec)	3240	3420	3600	3780	3960	4140	4320	4500	4680
Temp (°C)	37.91	37.13	36.24	35.46	34.81	34.04	33.5	32.85	32.31

Time (sec)	4860	5040	5220	5400	5580	5760	5940	6120	6300
Temp (°C)	31.77	31.23	30.81	30.38	29.84	29.52	29.1	28.78	28.35

Time (sec)	6480	6660	6840	7020	7200	7380	7560	7740	7920
Temp (°C)	28.04	27.61	27.4	27.08	26.87	26.66	26.34	26.13	25.91

Time (sec)	8100	8280	8460	8640	8820	9000	9180	9360	9540
Temp (°C)	25.7	25.49	25.28	25.07	24.96	24.75	24.54	24.43	24.22

Time (sec)	9720	9900	10080	10260	10440	10620	10800	10980	11160
Temp (°C)	24.11	23.9	23.79	23.69	23.47	23.37	23.26	23.15	23.05

Time (sec)	11340	11520	11700	11880	12060	12240	12420	12600	12780
Temp (°C)	22.94	22.83	22.83	22.62	22.51	22.51	22.41	22.41	22.3

Time (sec)	12960	13140	13320	13500	13680	13860	14040	14220
Temp (°C)	22.19	22.09	21.98	21.98	21.87	21.87	21.77	21.66

Home in the Dome

Have you ever thought about how you might calculate the volume inside a tent? In this activity you will use what you've learned in calculus to determine the volume of a dome-shaped tent.

Equipment Needed

- Hexagon-based dome-shaped tent
- Graphing calculator

Make whatever measurements you feel are necessary on the tent so that you can calculate the volume of the tent. Devise a method of checking your answer for reasonableness.

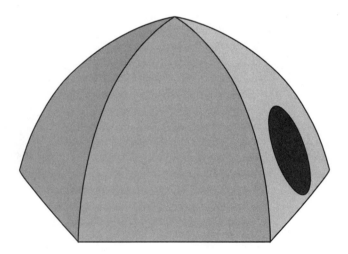

TEACHER NOTES 11
Home in the Dome

Prerequisite Knowledge

- How to find volumes by slicing
- How to find the area of a hexagon
- Data analysis skills (modeling a curve to fit data)

Equipment Needed

- Hexagon-based dome-shaped tent
- Graphing calculator

The objective of this lab is for students to apply to a real object the method of finding volumes by slicing. It is suitable for individual students or pairs. Measurements usually take less than 15 minutes. The calculations may take from less than one to up to three hours at the most, depending on some assumptions made and the general skills of the student(s). The lab works well as an extra assignment to be done out of class, perhaps for students who wish to do an extra credit project or as an additional assessment item. I set the tent up in the back corner of my classroom with a couple of meter sticks and tape measure nearby. Students come in and do the measuring during free time. Dome tents were very popular several years ago and can still be found in many camping and discount stores. For the purposes of the lab, it is not necessary to have a high-quality tent, only one that is dome-shaped.

Comments and Answers

Dome-shaped tents generally have a hexagonal base and stand about 1 meter tall. The support poles arch over the top in a roughly semicircular shape. Most students will model this curve with a semicircle, though some may use a semiellipse. In a rare case a student will model the curve with a catenary. The catenary is probably the most accurate curve, but the others work very well given that tents like this are never perfect in shape anyway. To calculate the volume, students need to find an equation for the area of a hexagon, $A(r)$, in terms of the radius (distance from center to vertex). Next, they need an equation for the curve of the support poles. Setting the origin of the coordinate system at the center of the base, let the x-axis run between the two ends of one pole and the y-axis run up through the top of the tent. Consider the volume of the tent to be made up of hexagonal layers parallel to the x-axis and perpendicular to the y-axis. The radius of each layer is then x. Integrate the area of a layer with respect to y to determine the volume. A small dome tent usually has a volume of about 1.5 cubic meters. Suggestions for verifying the volume usually involve filling the tent with foam packing peanuts or other such items and then transferring these to a box and measuring its volume.

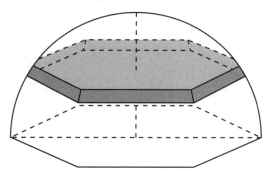

ACTIVITY *12*

H₂O in the S-K-Y

Your group is going to place a bid on painting the town water tower. Part of your score will be calculated by the formula Profit ÷ Bid Rank. Thus, a group that makes a bid with a $60 profit on the job but their bid comes in third will get a score of 20. A group with the lowest bid (bid rank of 1) who happens to lose $10 on the deal because they didn't plan on enough paint will earn a score of −10. Be very careful not to underbid the cost of materials as it will cause your group to get a negative score.

Equipment Needed

- Graphing calculator

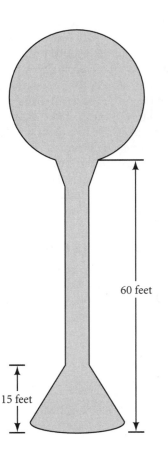

1. The township clerk is a little sketchy on details but has put this information down for all bidders: The spherical top holds a little over 54,000 gallons of water, the base of the top is 60 feet above the ground, and the diameter of the supporting column is one-third the radius of the sphere. The base of the supporting column flares out like a cone so that the diameter of the bottom is equal to the radius of the sphere; this bottom section is 15 feet tall. Likewise, the connection between the support and the sphere flares out to a diameter equal to two-thirds the radius of the sphere and is 10 feet tall.

2. The paint must be applied to an average thickness of 0.16 centimeters over the entire structure. You must calculate how much paint will be needed to paint the tower based on the details listed above. You also know that the paint will cost $47 a gallon wholesale when ordered in quantities of more than 20 gallons. Make your

60 feet

15 feet

A WATCHED CUP NEVER COOLS
© 1999 Key Curriculum Press

best bid. (If you have calculated wrong and we have to order more paint for you, it will cost $58 a gallon. Extra paint cannot be returned.) Since you already have all the other equipment needed for the job, your only cost will be for the paint.

3. Your report should include all calculations, equations, and diagrams needed to detail the design and determine the amount of paint needed. Explain your work. Be sure to include your bid for the job so that the town council (your teacher) can decide which group will receive the contract.

TEACHER NOTES 12
H$_2$0 in the S-K-Y

Prerequisite Knowledge

- How to find the volume of a sphere
- How to find the surface area of a cylinder
- How to find the surface area of a cone or frustum of a cone
- How to find the surface area by integration

Equipment Needed

- Graphing calculator

The objective of this lab is to provide students with a real-life situation in which to apply volumes and surface areas of revolution. In addition, the importance of accuracy, attention to detail, and appropriate use of units are inherent. The scoring comments in the lab are to encourage students to be accurate. This is an easy lab to make a mistake on and consequently come up with serious errors in the amount of paint to purchase. This competitive factor encourages students to check each calculation carefully to try to reduce these errors to a minimum.

This is a good lab for a small group of three or four students. It generally takes between one and two weeks outside of class. Since the groups are somewhat in competition, they like to work on their own, not in the classroom.

Comments and Answers

1. To hold 54,000 gallons of water or 7218.75 cubic feet, a sphere must have a radius of 11.99 feet. Students will probably use a radius of 12 feet for a volume of 54,145.7 gallons. If students do not have access to calculators with built-in conversion factors, you may wish to tell them that 1 gallon = 0.1336806 cubic feet. Once the radius has been determined, the rest of the dimensions are quite straightforward.

2. In calculating the surface area of the tower, students need to realize that the top is not a complete sphere. Rather, the conical support intersects the sphere and cuts off a portion. This is where the calculus comes in.

The rest of the surface area can be obtained with the formulas from geometry for the surface area of a cylinder and frustum of a cone. For the spherical portion, however, an integral is necessary. Once the surface area is known, the amount of paint can be calculated. Again if your students do not have access to calculators with built-in conversion factors, you may wish to give them some of this information:

$$1 \text{ inch} = 2.54 \text{ centimeters}$$

$$1 \text{ gallon} = 3785.4118 \text{ cubic centimeters}$$

$$1 \text{ cubic foot} = 1728 \text{ cubic inches}$$

Depending on what units they are using, they may need different conversion factors.

Surface area in square feet for each section of the tower in terms of r, the radius of the sphere:

Lower frustum $\quad \dfrac{2}{3}\pi r\sqrt{225 + \dfrac{r^2}{9}}$

Cylinder $\quad \dfrac{35}{3}\pi r$

Upper frustum $\quad \dfrac{1}{2}\pi r\sqrt{100 + \dfrac{r^2}{36}}$

Spherical portion $\quad 2\pi r^2\left(1 + \dfrac{\sqrt{35}}{36}\right)$

To convert to 20-gallon cans of paint, use the total surface area, S, in this formula:

$$S \cdot \frac{0.16 \text{ cm}}{(2.54 \text{ cm/in})(12 \text{ in/ft})} \cdot$$

$$\frac{1}{0.245424 \text{ft}^3/\text{gal}} \cdot \frac{1}{20 \text{ gal/can}}$$

Students should round this up to be sure to have enough paint. Multiply by $47 for the cost of the paint.

LAB ACTIVITY *13*

It Averages Out in the End

In this activity you will discover what it means to find the "average value" of a function. Then you will use this new definition to explore mean distances of the planets in our solar system from the sun.

PART **1**

A linear function

a. Graph the function $y = \frac{2}{3}x + 2$.

b. Complete the table below by tracing, evaluating the function, or using a table.

x	2.0	2.1	2.2	2.3	2.4	2.5	2.6	2.7	2.8	2.9	3.0
y											

c. Average the y-values in the table.

d. The region enclosed by the lines $x = 2$, $x = 3$, and $y = \frac{2}{3}x + 2$ is a trapezoid. Find the area of this trapezoid.

e. Compare the answers to 1c and 1d. How does the average found in 1c relate to the area of the region?

PART **2**

A semicircle

a. Graph the function $y = \sqrt{1 - x^2}$.

b. Complete the table below.

x	-1.0	-0.8	-0.6	-0.4	-0.2	0	0.2	0.4	0.6	0.8	1.0
y											

c. Average the y-values in the table.

d. Find the area of the semicircle using geometry.

e. The width of the interval is now 2. If you also consider this area to be equal to width multiplied by the average height, how can you use this average from 2c to approximate the area?

f. Use the same function and find the average of the *y* values of the function at every 0.1 within the interval. To make this calculation easier, use table functions or the program below with the equation in *y*1. (This program works with the TI-82, TI-83, TI-85, and TI-86.)

```
PROGRAM:AveVal
:Input "Left endpoint:",A
:Input "Right endpoint:",B
:Input "Step:",H
:0→S
:Int ((B-A)/H+1)→N
:For(x,A,B,H)
:S+y1→S
:End
:S/N→V
:Disp "Average value",V
```

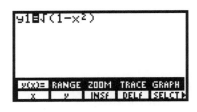

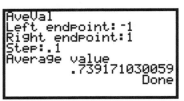

Run the program again with steps of 0.05, 0.01, and 0.005. Multiply these averages by the width, 2, and compare the result to the area you found in 2d. Explain your results.

PART 3

Another curve

a. Consider the function $y = 0.2x^3 - x^2 + 3$ over the interval $[1, 4]$. Add the following lines to the program listed in Part 2.

```
:V(B-A)→R
:Disp "Area",R
```

Use decreasing sizes of steps until you have determined the area to the nearest 0.01.

b. What is the "average" height of this function in this interval?

PART 4

Another curve

a. Use an integral to find the area in the region bounded by the *x*-axis, the lines $x = -3$, $x = 3$, and the curve $y = \sin x - 0.5x + 2$.

b.   Knowing the area under the curve, how can you find the "average" height of the function? What is the average height for the area in 4a?

c.   For any function $f(x)$ on the interval $[a, b]$, describe how you would calculate the average value.

d.   Explain why finding the average value using the integral is the same as averaging the function values for very small increments in x.

PART 5

An application of average value

The planets orbit around the sun in elliptical paths in which the sun is one of the two foci. The eccentricity of an ellipse is defined as the ratio of the focal length to the length of the semimajor axis.

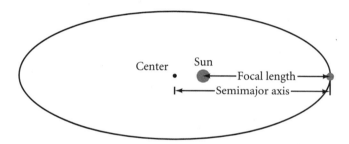

Given the eccentricity of each orbit and also the length of the semimajor axis for each planet, you can calculate the mean distance from the center of the system for each planet. Choose three planets and calculate the mean distance of each planet from the center of the solar system.

PLANET	SEMIMAJOR AXIS (AU)	ORBITAL ECCENTRICITY
Mercury	0.3871	0.206
Venus	0.7233	0.007
Earth	1.0000	0.017
Mars	1.5237	0.093
(Ceres)	2.7673	0.077
Jupiter	5.2028	0.048
Saturn	9.5388	0.056
Uranus	19.1820	0.047
Neptune	30.0580	0.009
Pluto	39.5177	0.249

TEACHER NOTES 13
It Averages Out in the End

Prerequisite Knowledge

- Formula for the area of a trapezoid
- Formula for the area of a semicircle
- How to find area by integration
- Equation of an ellipse
- Formula for the eccentricity of an ellipse
- Distance formula

The objective of this investigation is for students to discover the formula for the average value of a function and its meaning. This investigation can be done in pairs or with small groups or three or four students. It can also work as a whole class activity, with the last part assigned to small groups. The first two or three parts can be done in class during one period or assigned as out-of-class work. The fourth part extends the finite work from the first three parts to the continuous case and integration and would take part of a class period. Seeing the connection here helps students understand why the average value formula has its name. These first four parts of the investigation can be done in three or four days outside of class. The last part is an application of average value to a real setting. It could be omitted if you don't have enough time, but it should take only one or two days outside of class if the planets are distributed among group members.

Part 1
A linear function
a. The graph is a line whose slope is 2/3 with a y-intercept of 2.
b. Table values are as shown.

x	2.0	2.1	2.2	2.3	2.4	2.5
y	3.333	3.4	3.467	3.533	3.6	3.667

x	2.6	2.7	2.8	2.9	3.0
y	3.733	3.8	3.867	3.933	4.0

c. The average is 3.667.

d. The area of the trapezoid is
$\frac{1}{2}(1)(3.333 + 4) = 3.667$.
e. The answers are the same. The average found in 1c is equal to the area of the trapezoid.

Part 2
A semicircle
a. The graph is the upper semicircle of radius 1 centered at the origin.
b. Table values are as shown.

x	−1.0	−0.8	−0.6	−0.4	−0.2	0
y	0	0.6	0.8	0.917	0.980	1

x	0.2	0.4	0.6	0.8	1.0
y	0.980	0.917	0.8	0.6	0

c. The average is 0.696.
d. The area of the semicircle is $\frac{1}{2}(\pi)(1)^2 = 1.571$.
e. Multiply the average height, 0.696, by the width, 2, for an approximation.
$0.696 \cdot 2 = 1.392$
f. The average of the values with step 0.1 is 0.739, giving an area of 1.478.
The average of the values with step 0.05 is 0.763, giving an area of 1.526.
The average of the values with step 0.01 is 0.781, giving an area of 1.562.
The average of the values with step 0.005 is 0.783, giving an area of 1.566.

It appears that as the interval becomes smaller the average height multiplied by the width approaches the true area as a limit. This can be thought of as adding up many rectangles, each a small fraction of the width of the entire interval, with height determined by a value of the function. For example, in the original table, there were 11 function values. The calculation of the area could be rewritten as

$$\frac{1}{11}(2) \cdot 0 + \frac{1}{11}(2) \cdot 0.6 + \frac{1}{11}(2) \cdot 0.8 + \dots$$

$$+ \frac{1}{11}(2) \cdot 0.6 + \frac{1}{11}(2) \cdot 0$$

As the area under the curve is divided into more and more rectangles, the area approximation becomes better.

Part 3

Another curve

a. The actual area is 0.75 and can be found by integration. Using a step size of 0.005, the area is determined to be 0.754, which rounds to the correct value. Students may try other step sizes. Any step size that rounds to the correct value is acceptable. They should show a series of trials that move closer to the limit of 0.75.

b. The average height is 0.25, using the value found in 2a correct to two decimal places.

Part 4

Another curve

a. The area is 12.

b. Knowing the area, the average height can be found by dividing the area by the width of the interval. In this case, the average height is 2.

c. The average value is $\dfrac{\int_a^b f(x)\,dx}{b-a}$ or

$\dfrac{1}{b-a}\displaystyle\int_a^b f(x)\,dx$.

d. The definite integral adds up an infinite number of infinitely thin rectangles. Dividing the definite integral by the total width of all the rectangles results in the average of the heights. To make this clearer, consider an interval of width 6 divided into three sections. Suppose the heights of the three pieces are 3, 4, and 5. The sum of the areas is then $2(3) + 2(4) + 2(5)$ or 24. Dividing this by the total width, 6, gives an answer of 4, which is the average of the three original heights. Similarly, dividing the definite integral by the width gives the average of an infinite number of function values.

Part 5

An application of average value

To calculate the mean distance from the center of the solar system for each planet, you must first find the equation for the path of each planet. To do so, calculate the length of the semiminor axis, $b = \sqrt{a^2 - c^2}$. The distance from the center of the system is given by the equation

$s = \sqrt{x^2 + b^2\left(1 - \dfrac{x^2}{a^2}\right)}$. Integrating this function

over the interval from $-a$ to a and dividing by $2a$ gives the average value.

PLANET	MEAN DISTANCE FROM CENTER
Mercury	0.38158
Venus	0.72329
Earth	0.99990
Mars	1.5193
(Ceres)	2.7618
Jupiter	5.1988
Saturn	9.5288
Uranus	19.1679
Neptune	30.0572
Pluto	38.6906

LAB ACTIVITY *14*

Square Pegs in Round Holes

In this activity you will look at different ways to approximate an area bounded by a curve. Then you will apply these methods to determine how much water is flowing through a stream in one hour.

Equipment Needed

- Graphing calculator
- Measuring tape
- Measuring sticks
- A nearby stream or river (or sample data from the teacher's manual)

PART 1

Following are two graphs of the function $f(x) = \frac{1}{x}$. The x-interval $[1, 5]$ has been subdivided into four equal-width subintervals. On the left, four rectangles are drawn whose heights are determined by the value of the function at the right end of each subinterval. On the right, four trapezoids are drawn that approximate the area under the curve for this interval.

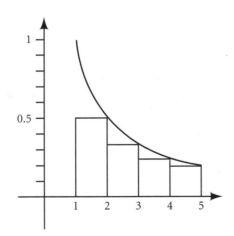 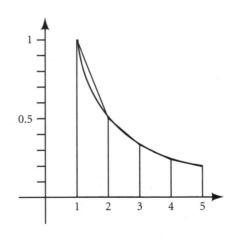

   a. Determine the sum of the areas of the four rectangles.

   b. Determine the sum of the areas of the four trapezoids.

   c. Rewrite the rectangular sum in general form for n rectangles using a as the leftmost x-value, b as the rightmost x-value and h as the width of each subinterval. For the x-values in between use

$$a = x_0 < x_1 < x_2 < \ldots < x_{n-1} < x_n = b$$

PART 2

The next graph shows a function f on the interval $[a, b]$. The interval is divided into four equal-width subintervals.

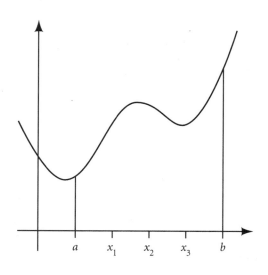

   a. Draw the trapezoids for the trapezoid approximation using these four subintervals.

   b. Using this subdivision of $[a, b]$, write an expression for T_4, the trapezoid approximation using four subintervals. The formula for the sum of the areas should be written in terms of h, $f(x_0)$, $f(x_1)$, $f(x_2)$, $f(x_3)$, and $f(x_4)$, where h is the width of an interval.

   c. Divide the interval $[a, b]$ into n equal-length subintervals using the points $a = x_0 < x_1 < x_2 < \ldots < x_{n-1} < x_n = b$. Then, generalize your results from 2b to determine an expression for T_n (the trapezoid approximation using n subintervals).

PART 3

While trapezoids provide a better approximation than rectangles, you are still trying to fit the area under a curve with a straight line. In the long run the trapezoids will fit pretty well, but it seems more efficient to fit a curve with a curve. The simplest curve to work with is the parabola. The following steps will lead you to develop a formula for finding the area under a curve with a series of parabola-topped sections.

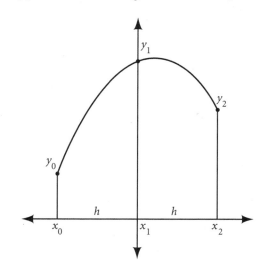

a. Study the figure. Find the area under the curve $y = Ax^2 + Bx + C$ in the interval $[-h, h]$ by integrating.

b. What are the values for y_0, y_1, y_2 in terms of A, B, C, and h? Just as there are formulas for the areas of triangles, rectangles, and trapezoids, there is a formula for the area under a parabola that does not depend on integration. That expression is $n(y_0 + y_2) + my_1$. Find values for n and m in terms of h to make this expression equal to the one you found in 3a.

c. Rewrite the expression for the area under the curve using your values for n and m in terms of y_0, y_1, and y_2.

d. If y_0, y_1, y_2 are the values of any function, then the area under the parabola provides an approximation for the area under the original function. If the interval $[a, b]$ is divided into six subintervals, how many parabolic segments will be used to approximate the area under the curve? Write the expressions for the areas of these parabolic sections in terms of h, $y_0, y_1, \ldots, y_6$. Then combine all of these expressions into one.

e. Generalize your results from 3d to approximate the area under the curve for n subdivisions of the interval. Note any restrictions on n you discover.

PART 4

The approximation method you developed in Part 3 is called Simpson's method, even though it was known long before Thomas Simpson was born. Compare the accuracy of the trapezoidal method and Simpson's method for the following functions and the given numbers of subdivisions.

n	TRAPEZOIDAL APPROXIMATION	SIMPSON'S APPROXIMATION	
$y = \sin x \,[0, \pi]$			Actual Area $= 2$
2			
4			
8			
$y = \dfrac{1}{x}\,[1, 3]$			Actual Area $= \ln 3$ ≈ 1.098612289
2			
4			
8			
16			

Discuss the accuracy of the two methods. What are the advantages and disadvantages of each one?

PART 5

a. Measure the depth of a stream at even intervals across its width. Record these values and make a sketch of the cross section of the stream at your measuring spot. Also, record the width of the stream. Determine the speed of the current by timing the float of a ping-pong ball down a measured length of the stream.

b. Approximate the area of this cross section using a rectangular method, the trapezoidal method, and Simpson's method. Pay careful attention to units. Explain any unit conversions you perform. Based on these figures, what is your best estimate for the cross-sectional area of the stream? Justify your estimate.

c. Using your information on the current speed and your answer from 5b, determine the amount of water flowing through the stream in one hour. Once again, pay careful attention to units.

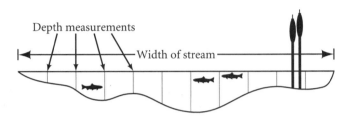

Data for Activity 14: Square Pegs in Round Holes

The data below was collected in January from the Little Betsie River in Interlochen, Michigan.

WIDTH (FT)	DEPTH (IN.)	WIDTH (FT)	DEPTH (IN.)	WIDTH (FT)	DEPTH (IN.)
0	0.25	12	7.25	24	27.5
1	4.5	13	7.0	25	31.25
2	8.0	14	9.0	26	33.75
3	10.5	15	10.5	27	34.25
4	10.5	16	13.25	28	35.75
5	10.5	17	13.5	29	37.0
6	11.5	18	15.0	30	36.25
7	10.25	19	16.0	31	33.0
8	10.5	20	17.0	32	29.0
9	10.0	21	19.5	33	24.25
10	8.25	22	24.5	34	17.5
11	8.75	23	27.5		

A ping-pong ball floated a distance of 20 feet down the stream. The times for four trips are 21, 18.9, 17, and 16 seconds, respectively.

TEACHER NOTES 14
Square Pegs in Round Holes

Prerequisite Knowledge

- How to approximate the area under a curve with rectangles
- How to find the area of a trapezoid
- Integration of polynomials

Equipment Needed

- Graphing calculator
- Measuring sticks and tapes
- A nearby river or stream (or the sample data provided)

In this exploration students compare rectangular approximations of area with approximations using trapezoids and finally the parabolically topped pieces of Simpson's method. Students should be familiar with the rectangular methods before beginning this investigation. They should also be able to find areas using definite integrals for polynomials. The entire lab takes up to two weeks outside of class and is most suitable for small groups. The first three parts go quite quickly. The derivation of Simpson's rule is more difficult. Check up on students' progress through this part. The comparison of methods in Part 5 should show students that though the techniques converge at different rates, they all reach the same limit, the actual area. The final portions of this lab are an application of the techniques to a real-life situation. If a stream is not accessible for collecting data, use the provided sample data set. With the availability of computers and even calculators that can perform analytic integration on almost any given function, this application points out the need for numeric techniques. There is no known function for the stream bottom. Working from numerical data is the only way to determine this cross-sectional area.

Comments and Answers

Part 1

a. The sum of the areas of the four rectangles is 1.2833.

b. The sum of the areas of the four trapezoids is 1.6833.

c. $\frac{1}{x_1} \cdot \frac{b-a}{n} + \frac{1}{x_2} \cdot \frac{b-a}{n} + \ldots + \frac{1}{x_n} \cdot \frac{b-a}{n}$ or

$\sum_{k=1}^{n} \left(\frac{1}{x_k} \cdot \frac{b-a}{n} \right)$ or

$f(x_1) \cdot \frac{b-a}{n} + f(x_2) \cdot \frac{b-a}{n} + \ldots + f(x_n) \cdot \frac{b-a}{n}$

or any equivalent expression for the sum of the areas of n rectangles.

Part 2

a.

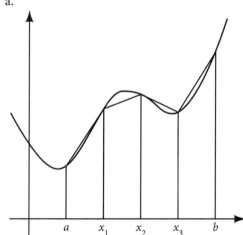

b. $\frac{1}{2}h[\,f(x_0) + f(x_1)] + \frac{1}{2}h[\,f(x_1) + f(x_2)]$
$+ \frac{1}{2}h[\,f(x_2) + f(x_3)] + \frac{1}{2}h[\,f(x_3) + f(x_4)]$ or
$\frac{1}{2}h[\,f(x_0) + 2f(x_1) + 2f(x_2) + 2f(x_3) + f(x_4)]$
Students should explain how their formula was developed, showing all steps.

c. $T_n = \frac{1}{2}h[\,f(x_0) + 2f(x_1) + 2f(x_2) + \ldots$
$+ 2f(x_{n-1}) + f(x_n)]$ or

$T_n = \frac{1}{2}h \sum_{k=1}^{n} f(x_{k-1}) + f(x_k)$

Students should explain how their formula was developed. They need not use sigma notation for the final answer.

Part 3

The derivation that follows is not easy. Encourage students to work together. Check up on their progress before they proceed to Part 4.

a.
$$\int_{-h}^{h} (Ax^2 + Bx + C)\, dx = \left[\tfrac{1}{3}Ax^3 + \tfrac{1}{2}Bx^2 + Cx\right]_{-h}^{h}$$
$$= \left[\tfrac{1}{3}Ah^3 + \tfrac{1}{2}Bh^2 + Ch + \tfrac{1}{3}Ah^3 - \tfrac{1}{2}Bh^2 + Ch\right]$$
$$= \left[\tfrac{2}{3}Ah^3 + 2Ch\right] = 2h\left(\tfrac{1}{3}Ah^2 + C\right)$$

b. $y_0 = Ah^2 - Bh + C,\ y_1 = C,$
$y_2 = Ah^2 + Bh + C$
$$n(y_0 + y_2) + my_1 =$$
$$n(Ah^2 - Bh + C + Ah^2 + Bh + C) + mC$$
$$= n(2Ah^2 + 2C) + mC$$
$$n(2Ah^2 + 2C) + mC = 2h\left(\tfrac{1}{3}Ah^2 + C\right)$$
$$2nh^2A + (2n + m)C = \tfrac{2}{3}h^3A + 2hC \text{ so}$$
$$n = \tfrac{1}{3}h \text{ and } m = \tfrac{4}{3}h$$

c. $n(y_0 + y_2) + my_1 = \tfrac{1}{3}h(y_0 + y_2) + \tfrac{4}{3}hy_1$

d. For six subintervals, you will need three parabolic segments.
$$\tfrac{1}{3}h(y_0 + y_2) + \tfrac{4}{3}hy_1 + \tfrac{1}{3}h(y_2 + y_4) + \tfrac{4}{3}hy_3$$
$$+ \tfrac{1}{3}h(y_4 + y_6) + \tfrac{4}{3}hy_5$$

By combining like terms and removing common factors, this expression becomes
$$\tfrac{1}{3}h(y_0 + 4y_1 + 2y_2 + 4y_3 + 2y_4 + 4y_5 + y_6).$$

e. $\tfrac{1}{3}h(y_0 + 4y_1 + 2y_2 + 4y_3 + \ldots + 2y_{n-2} + 4y_{n-1} + y_n$

The value of n must be even since each parabolic segment is made from two of the subintervals.

Part 4

The values for the various approximations are shown below. Students will probably do these calculations by hand, but they may also program the calculator to do them.

Both the trapezoidal and Simpson's approximations approach the actual areas in the limit. The Simpson's approximation is closer to the limit for a smaller number of subdivisions. However, to use Simpson's method, you must have an even number of subdivisions, which might be a disadvantage. It is also a slightly more complicated formula to remember and derive. The trapezoidal formula is easier to reconstruct if you forget it, and works with any number of subdivisions. However, you must use a large number of subdivisions to get the accuracy you get with a small n in Simpson's formula.

n	TRAPEZOIDAL APPROXIMATION	SIMPSON'S APPROXIMATION	
$y = \sin x\ [0, \pi]$			Actual Area $= 2$
2	1.5708	2.0944	
4	1.8961	2.005	
8	1.9742	2.0003	
$y = \tfrac{1}{x}\ [1, 3]$			Actual Area $= \ln 3$ ≈ 1.098612289
2	1.1667	1.1111	
4	1.1167	1.1000	
8	1.1032	1.0987	
16	1.0998	1.0986	

Part 5

a. Any size stream will work for this portion of the investigation, from something a few feet wide to a small river 30 or 40 feet in width. If you don't have a stream nearby, some actual data are provided on a blackline master. If using a large stream, check to see that the current is not too swift or the stream too deep. Chest-waders may be needed. For a very small stream, rubber boots may suffice. Stretch a tape measure across the width of the stream. At evenly spaced intervals, measure the depth with a yardstick or ruler. You may want to attach a flat piece of wood to the bottom of the stick to prevent it sinking into the bottom.

b. Students should be very careful to work with consistent units. The various estimates will probably be very similar. Students will generally prefer the Simpson's estimate.

c. Multiply the speed of the current by the cross-sectional area to get the volume of water flowing through the stream. Again, students need to be careful to make the correct conversions to get the amount of water flowing through the stream in one hour.

LAB ACTIVITY 15

As Easy as π

Did you know that you can use calculus to find the volumes of some everyday objects? In this activity you will develop a method for finding the volume of a circular object that is not a simple geometric shape such as a cone or cylinder.

Equipment Needed

- Circular pie pan
- Graphing calculator

Step 1 Choose a pie pan from the selection provided.

Step 2 Measure all dimensions and record them. Also make and label a sketch of the pan.

Step 3 Estimate the volume by calculating the volume of two short cylindrical layers that would approximately fill the pan.

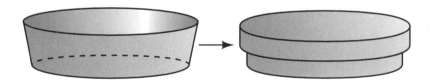

Step 4 Improve your estimate by using four layers.

Step 5 Improve your estimate by using a larger number of layers of your choice.

Step 6 As you divide the volume into more layers, each layer becomes thinner. If you were to continue this process, generating estimates with more and more very, very thin layers, what do you predict that the limit for the volume would be?

Step 7 Using the dimensions and data on your pan, find an equation for the radius of the pan in terms of the height. (You may have already done this.)

Step 8   Write an expression that indicates summing up an infinite number of infinitely thin layers. How does this result compare to the estimates you found in Steps 3, 4, and 5?

Step 9   Use your method from Step 8 to write an expression for the volume of the object shown below.

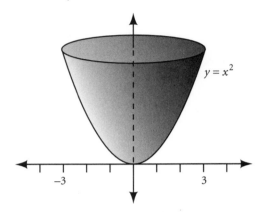

$y = x^2$

-3 3

TEACHER NOTES 15
As Easy as π

Prerequisite Knowledge

- Formula for the volume of a cylinder
- Integration of polynomials
- Understanding of integration as the summation of an infinite number of infinitely small things

Equipment Needed

- Assorted circular pie pans
- Graphing calculator

In this exploration, students develop the disk method of determining a volume of revolution. It is best done in pairs and can be completed within a class period. Have an assortment of pie pans available for your students—one pan per pair is ideal. Once measurements are made and recorded, pans may be passed to another group. However, it is better if students are able to keep the pan in front of them to help visualize the process as the exploration develops. Number the pie pans in some fashion; that way you can see if their measurements are reasonable. A sample data set is not provided for this lab. I have at least six different types of pie pans in my cupboard. All purport to be 8, 9, or 10 inches. However, no two actually have the same measurements. A quick check of volume for a specific pan can be made in your chemistry lab by filling the pan with water from a graduated cylinder or burette. Ordinary household measuring cups vary widely in their actual volumes and trying to use them to verify the volume of a pan can be very unreliable.

A sample student lab report follows.

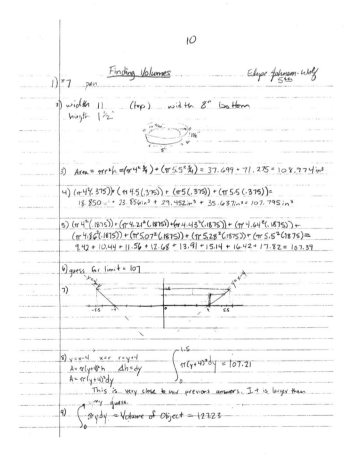

LAB ACTIVITY 16

Let the Games Begin!

Why do you think that many sports stadiums are round? Often large sports stadiums also have domed ceilings. Of course, the owners of these stadiums want to be able to accommodate as many people as possible, but the people like to be able to get to their seats without having to climb over too many other people. There are also fire and safety regulations that affect how many stairways and aisles there must be. In this activity you will design a sports stadium given certain criteria.

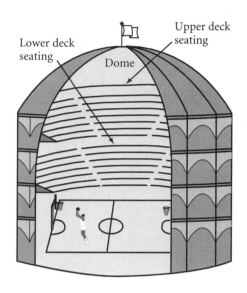

Equipment Needed

- Graphing calculator
- Access to performance space such as auditorium (optional)

Your task is to design a sports stadium that has a capacity of at least 15,000 seats that meets the criteria listed below.

- The outer boundary of the stadium is circular.
- There are two tiers of seating, both of which are on curves.
- The playing area must be large enough to hold a standard basketball court.
- The ceiling must be dome-shaped.
- You may decided how many stairways and aisles to include, but remember, people don't like to have to climb over too many others to get to their seats. Measure seats, aisles, and stairways in at least one performance space to determine the amount of area these will occupy in your design.

When submitting your design, include all equations and calculations used. Determine the number of seats in your stadium and the surface area of the domed ceiling. Also, determine the volume of air inside the stadium, since ventilation will be a major element in the final building plans. Scale drawings or models will be accepted as part of your design presentation, but you will also need written documentation.

TEACHER NOTES 16
Let the Games Begin!

Prerequisite Knowledge

- How to determine the volume and surface area by integration (geometry for the simplified version of the project)

Equipment Needed

- Graphing calculator
- Access to a performance space such as an auditorium (optional)

The objective of this project is to give students a chance to apply techniques for finding volumes of solids of revolution and surface area, as well as practical considerations. This is a long-term project, best done in groups of three or four students. It could accompany the entire study of volumes and surfaces of revolution, with students doing parts of the design throughout the entire unit and then taking another week or two outside of class to put the final project together. The tiers of seats can be modeled on variations of $y = 1/x$. In determining the number of seats, students can take the surface area of the seating tier and subtract the area needed for stairways or aisles. Then divide the remaining area by the amount needed for one seat, including leg room. This simplification will probably result in a number of seats that is larger than would actually fit, but should suffice. Taking some measurements in the school auditorium and a local theater or arena should give sufficient data to complete this portion of the project. In determining the volume of air in the stadium, students can choose to completely ignore the upper tier of seating, or adjust for this by finding the volume in sections. The space below the lower tier can also be ignored, if desired, making the volume simply a cylinder and portion of a sphere. The more simplifications you make, the easier the problem and the less time it will take to complete the project.

LAB ACTIVITY 17

Focus on Food

Satellite dishes and headlights both work because of the reflection properties of a parabola. When parallel rays such as radio waves, coming from far away, strike the sides of a parabola, they are reflected through the focus, thus being concentrated and picked up by the microphone placed at the focus of the satellite dish. When a signal is sent out from the focus, it reflects off the sides of the parabola, moving out in parallel beams. In the same way, the light from the bulb in a headlight is sent out directly in front of the car.

Another use of a parabolic surface can be to concentrate the rays of the sun to apply heat to a specific point. You will explore this application in this project.

Your task is to design and construct a parabolic dish solar cooker. The dish should be no more than 1 meter in diameter. The dish should have some way of placing a food item at the focus for cooking. Your cooker will be tested on a sunny day by placing a marshmallow at the focus and measuring the temperature at its center.

A WATCHED CUP NEVER COOLS
© 1999 Key Curriculum Press

TEACHER NOTES 17
Focus on Food

Prerequisite Knowledge

- Equation of a parabola

Equipment Needed

- A wide variety, depending on students' choices

In this project students design and build their own parabolic dish for cooking marshmallows. The project as described does not use any calculus. However, if a written report is required, students can be asked to calculate the surface area of their dish and the volume inside it, and also develop a technique to evaluate the accuracy of their construction. A group of three to six students works well for this project. Since no specific construction instructions are given, students must work together to come up with a design, starting with an equation. This project is an exercise in working together and listening to each other. In the past, my students have constructed dishes from chicken wire and papier maché, wire, poster board, wooden doweling, and wire and duct tape on a plywood backing. In all cases they used lots of aluminum foil for their designs. In areas with more direct sunlight than northern Michigan you may wish to limit the size to less than half a meter. In areas with less sun, the true test is the temperature inside the marshmallow. Test all dishes under the same conditions, perhaps during a lunch hour or after school.

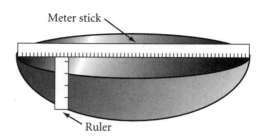

Meter stick

Ruler

When evaluating the dishes, place a temperature probe at the center of the marshmallow. Even on a cloudy day it will heat up slightly. In addition to measuring the final temperature, observe how long it takes for the marshmallows to heat up. To test for how accurately they have created a parabolic shape, measure the dishes as shown above and then fit their equations to the data points.

A suggested rubric for assessing students' work is given below. The point values are only suggested and can be modified to fit any range desired.

CATEGORY	POSSIBLE
Meets specification of design	3
Ability to hold shape	3
Ease of orientation and use	3
Achieves cooking temperature	3
Group cooperation	3
Group organization	3
Efficient use of time and materials	3
Problem-solving efficiency	3
Appearance	1
Total	**25**

LAB ACTIVITY 18

Lights, Camera, Action!

Choose one or, even better, several related concepts and create a problem that incorporates them in its solution. Present the problem on videotape. This performance may include animation, pictures of a calculator screen, live action, music, or any other creative features. All members of the group should participate in the presentation in some way, but they all do not have to appear on screen. The video must be between 10 and 25 minutes in length. Use the timetable below to keep your progress on schedule.

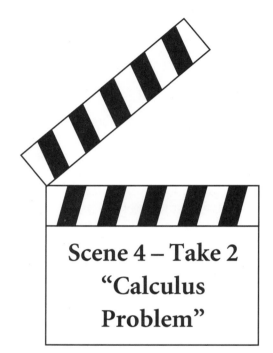

Scene 4 – Take 2
"Calculus Problem"

STAGE OF COMPLETION	DATE
Description of the problem	
Basic concept of the video	
Problem solutions and props	
Final video	

The video will be graded using the criteria listed below.

Breadth and depth of content covered: Did your presentation use a variety of concepts? Did you use a variety of solution techniques? Did you extend the problem to its fullest?

Clarity of presentation: How well could your presentation be understood with only one viewing? Was the narration or writing clear? Was enough time allowed for those watching to absorb the material?

Correctness of mathematics: Were there no mathematical errors? Was the solution correct in all aspects?

Entertainment or creative aspects: Was your presentation enjoyable to watch? Were there artistic aspects? Did it incorporate humor? Did it take a different approach rather than just a traditional look at the problem?

TEACHER NOTES 18
Lights, Camera, Action!

Prerequisite Knowledge

- As much mathematics as possible

Equipment Needed

- Video equipment
- Will vary with individual projects

This lab gives students the chance to be creative and show just how much they have learned. It is an excellent end-of-the-course project. It is designed to be a video presentation, but could be done as a live presentation, a multimedia computer project, or a written paper. Plan on two weeks or more for this project. The timetable provided in the text is useful for keeping students on track. Allow up to a week for the first stage of completion, "Description of the problem." At this point students should have determined the basic problem setting and extensions they wish to investigate. They do not have to have all aspects of the problem solved or even have settled on the plan for the video, but they do need to have a clear direction. Be sure that the group has created a problem that has enough depth and richness so that they will be able to show a variety of skills and content. Allow only a couple of more days before the second stage of completion, "Basic concept of the video." At this point students should have a plan of how to present the problem. This may mean a story line or order of presentation laid out. Three or four more days should be sufficient to reach the third stage of completion, "Problem solutions and props." At this point all aspects of the problem should be solved and the students should be ready to film or otherwise assemble the presentation. Depending on the availability of equipment and the methods students will use to make the problem presentations, they will need different amounts of time.

Once all the presentations are complete, be sure to schedule a Calculus Film Festival or other event so that all students, and hopefully those from other classes as well, will have a chance to see the top presentations.

LAB ACTIVITY *19*

The Cup

You have been given an object that will hold liquid.
Your task is to determine as much as possible about
this object. Your report must include those items
listed below.

1. The volume that the object will hold.
2. The inner surface area of the object.
3. The amount of work needed to empty the object
   of water by pumping it over the edge.
4. If water is being poured in at a constant rate of
   2 cubic centimeters per second, at what rate is
   the water level rising when the object contains
   half its volume?
5. Include any other information or properties that
   you can determine about the object. Try to include
   some additional mathematical facts. Be creative.
   Write as much as you can for this section.

   Use the timetable below to keep track of your progress.

STAGE OF COMPLETION	DATE
Equations developed	
First four questions answered	
Extra information collected	
Report complete	

TEACHER NOTES 19
The Cup

Prerequisite Knowledge

- Data analysis skills (modeling data with one or more equations)
- How to find volume and surface area, and work by integration
- Related rates
- As much other mathematics as possible

Equipment Needed

- Object that holds liquid—one for each small group (plastic champagne or wine glass, bottle)

This is an excellent end-of-the-year project that asks students to apply everything they have learned throughout the course. It is best done in small groups of three or four students. Alternatively, the project could be done in stages throughout the year as each topic is covered. Each group should be given a plastic wine or champagne glass. These are readily available at party supply stores. Look for glasses with interesting shapes and with no sharp breaks in the curve of the side. This shape gives students the most options in fitting curves to the shape. There are no absolutely correct answers here. Modeling a real object is a true challenge. Students should be encouraged to use a piecewise-defined function. The first challenge is to take measurements of the cup. My students have used a wide variety of methods. One technique is to fill the cup with modeling clay. However, removing it without distorting the shape is difficult. Other students have laid a string soaked with starch along the curve. When dry it can be removed and traced onto graph paper. Another technique has been to measure the circumference of the cup at regular intervals and then calculate a radius for each point. Still another technique was to photograph the cup and then take measurements off of the print. In short, there are many very creative ways to do this. Try not to give too many hints; coming up with their own technique is a great victory for students. Allow at least two weeks for the completion of this project. The timetable should be used to keep students on track. The first stage, "Equations developed," takes

the most time. A week is usually sufficient, although students may modify their equations at a later time. The second stage, "First four questions answered," will take two or three more days. The third stage, "Extra information collected," will take a day or two, depending on how ambitious the students are. The last stage, "Report complete," should take only a day or two, provided students have been writing various parts of their reports as they are completed.

Volume: Most students will use calculus to find the volume and then verify their answers by actually filling the cup. Others will simply determine the volume by filling the cup with water. That's fine; there will be plenty of calculus in the other sections.

Surface area: The inner surface area is specified since some cups have a fluted outer edge which would complicate the outer surface area calculations.

Work: If students did not find the volume using the disk method, they will need to do very similar calculations here. If work was not studied, then omit this section and require the volume to be done using calculus.

Related rate: In solving this portion of the problem students usually rediscover the fundamental theorem of calculus. Since the volume is determined by an integral, and they need the rate of change of the volume, the fundamental theorem is used.

Additional information: This is time for more creativity. Students often find such things as the mass of the cup, the density, and chemical formula for the plastic. In addition they may find the center of mass of the cup or other physical properties. Along a more humorous line, students often determine the number of popcorn kernels it takes to fill the cup or how far they can walk with cups balanced on their heads. Musical students may try to find the pitch of the cup. Some students may try to see how much weight the plastic glass will support before it breaks (which is quite a lot if the load is carefully placed on the top of the cup), or try to determine the probability of it landing on its side or top if dropped from a certain height.

WRITING ASSIGNMENTS

WRITING ASSIGNMENTS

Note to Students

Your responses to the writing assignments will vary in length and type. Some assignments ask you to interpret calculus or mathematical concepts using nonmathematical language or to find examples of these concepts in nonmathematical contexts. Other assignments ask you to delve more deeply into the concepts and ideas themselves and to justify or explain some of the fine points that you may not have considered previously. Or you may be asked for your personal reflections and thoughts. On all of the assignments, take the time to write and rewrite. Many of the questions involve more than you may originally imagine. A second or third look at the question and your answer may be helpful. Feel free to consult textbooks, teachers, peers, or other sources when doing any of these writing assignments.

TEACHER NOTES
Writing Assignments

These assignments can be used in a variety of ways. One way is to assign them at the time the topic is being studied, then let students turn in an initial draft partway through the unit. This will give you insight into their current understanding. Write comments on the papers and have students rewrite them at least once more before a final version is submitted. Alternatively, the papers may be assigned after the unit is complete. This gives students the opportunity to reflect on what they have learned and writing the papers reinforces what they have learned. Allowing students to rewrite assignments adds to their understanding. However, some assignments are suitable for a single writing. In all writing, look for clarity of language, precision of mathematical ideas, and good mechanics. Examples of almost every writing assignment are included along with comments regarding strengths that they demonstrate.

Writing in and about mathematics may be a new activity for some of your students. To help students learn what you want them to learn, try reading portions of good writing to them. Distribute copies of good papers from some of your students for their study. Another idea is to put portions of papers on the overhead and use them as discussion starters for class. Visit with the English teachers for other suggestions on how to encourage good writing habits.

WRITING ASSIGNMENT *1*

Mathematics and Me

Write your mathematical autobiography. Use the questions listed below to help guide your narrative.

Your earliest memories of mathematics or numbers

Your elementary and junior high experiences

- Did mathematics come easily to you?
- Did you enjoy it?
- What were your favorite activities?
- What are your most memorable mathematical experiences from these grades?

Your high school experiences

- What were your courses in algebra, geometry, and precalculus like?
- Did you have any "bad" years or units?
- What gaps or weaknesses do you think you are bringing with you?
- What are your strengths?
- Did you like these courses?
- Did you have any unusual courses?
- How hard did you work?
- Did the material come easily or did you have to study a lot?
- Were you involved in mathematics competitions?

Calculator/computer experiences

- Have you used graphing calculators or computers in mathematics classes?
- Were they used often and in what way?
- How did you feel about these experiences?

Your expectations for this year

- Why did you sign up for calculus?

- What do you expect the year to be like?

- Do you have plans for after high school that involve mathematics or science-related fields?

Throughout this paper, please emphasize your personal experiences and feelings. Be thorough. Pay attention to grammar, spelling, and general writing habits. This paper will be used to assist me in getting to know you individually and to plan the first few weeks of class. Please be honest. Everything you write will be kept confidential between us.

TEACHER NOTES 1
Mathematics and Me

This is a personal reflection from the student. It can be very helpful in spotting students who will need extra help and those who can be expected to be leaders. You will also begin to spot the creative minds and those who may shine in some nontraditional roles. Look for thoroughness as well as good writing skills in this paper.

WRITING ASSIGNMENT 2

A Function by Any Other Name

In this assignment you will compare a nonmathematical definition of a term used in mathematics with a mathematical one.

- Write a nonmathematical definition of "function," and describe how you might use this word outside of mathematics. Avoid using a dictionary definition. Think about how you use the word in everyday language.

- Write a mathematical definition of "function" in your own words—not the definition you found in your mathematics textbook.

- Compare the two definitions you wrote. What similarities are there? How are they different?

    Be as complete as possible in your discussion.

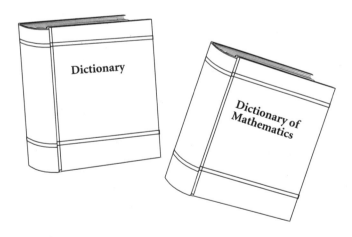

A WATCHED CUP NEVER COOLS
© 1999 Key Curriculum Press

TEACHER NOTES 2
A Function by Any Other Name

This assignment could be used in a journal format or as a minor paper. It can also be given several times throughout a student's mathematics career. The concept of function is central to mathematics and by repeating this assignment it will become more vital and real to a student. In this assignment students are asked to consider their definition of the word "function." Most will start with the dictionary, but ask them to think on a more personal level. What does it mean to them? How do they use the word. Then students describe their mathematical understanding. At the beginning, this may be a fairly rote recital of a math book definition. However, don't be satisfied with this. The more they think about this concept and ponder it, the deeper their understanding. This is a paper that is definitely worth writing and rewriting. In grading, look for clarity of expression and accuracy of detail. The depth of understanding will vary from student to student; look for as much as they can give at their current level.

Alysia Williams
10/5/96

A Function by Any Other Name

Freshman World History - Mr. Peters's class. We were learning about the Athenians and the Spartans when I first heard the idea of form versus function used. The Athenians were artists and intellectuals, and designed their world to show the way their minds worked. The result was high, awe-inspiring architecture, intricate and breathtaking in design. Their buildings served their function (to shelter people from the elements, to serve as a place of worship, etc.), but they also served toward another end: the buildings were created for decoration almost as much as for shelter.

From the Spartans, I learned the idea of function. The Spartans were a military people. They had no time to waste on adding Corinthian flourishes to a pillar; just so long as the thing held the building up, the Spartans were happy. Everything did exactly what it was supposed to - nothing more. No bells and whistles (hence we get the term "Spartan"). This is what I've learned to be the "real life" definition of the term "function": something that works in the manner intended without any added fuss. For example: a closet is meant to hold things. In Thor Johnson Hall, the closets do just that (but barely). At least in my room, the builders never bothered themselves with putting anything superfluous on the closet - like doors. The builders obviously thought that doors weren't needed, since doors do nothing for the original intention of the closets (to hold things). According to the definition,

---

then, my closet is functional (or "Spartan").

A mathematical definition of "function," would be a picture or equation in which the activity can be seen and/or predicted. For every x value, there is a subsequent y value (but only one). For example: in a graph of a line, one can see that where the line is going, and make educated guesses on what the line is doing outside of the graph based on what can be seen. In the equation of a line, the activity is more easily predicted: just plug in a value for x, and a y value will come out. The same is true for any function, no matter how complicated. Functions are nice things. Whatever is in the equation, they do. If the x is raised to the third power, the graph will have two curves. There are no loops to worry about.

These two definitions are the same, in the sense that a function does what it needs to do, and leaves out the frills. In real life, the frills may be lacy curtains or doors on a closet. In math, the frills appear in the form of extra y values.

The first difference between the two, is that in real life one can't always tell right away if something is functional or not. At first glance, most people would think that closet doors are necessary - a given, if you will. But if they truly are functional, then if they are missing, a closet is rendered useless. My closet still works (for all the world to see), so doors are not functional. In a graph, a simple vertical line test will tell if the picture is a function or not. In an equation, if the y is squared, the equation is not a function,

---

because two values for y will be found. Another difference, is that in real life, things can be both round and functional - like a wheel. Of course, one might go so far as to argue the necessity of wheels on a car, but that's a whole other writing assignment entirely...

Could have explored the mathematical definition of function more completely, but otherwise an enjoyable and thoughtful piece of writing

19

WRITING ASSIGNMENT 3

Take It to the Limit

While limits are a fundamental concept in calculus, the idea of a limit can be found elsewhere. Music, visual arts, advertising, and other areas of popular culture often use the concept. Find an example of a song, poem, picture, or other item and explain how it uses or demonstrates the concept of a limit.

A WATCHED CUP NEVER COOLS
© 1999 Key Curriculum Press

TEACHER NOTES 3
Take It to the Limit

Introduce this assignment with the song of the same name by the Eagles. Students may have heard this before, but for many of them it will be new. Discuss how the lyrics describe a limit. The singer finds himself drawn to thoughts of someone and no matter what happens he keeps coming back to her. This is a limit. A function tends toward a value and no matter what, as x approaches a value c, the function approaches the limiting value L. Other examples exist in music, both popular and classical. In art, limits can be seen in perspective drawing, mixing of colors, and the lightness and darkness of shades of colors. Similar concepts exist in everything from toothpaste (can you ever reach the limit of getting it all out of the tube?) to the temperature of your shower (you keep turning it up, just how hot can it get? how hot can you stand?) to falling asleep (can you identify the point in time where you actually fall asleep?) This paper may take students a while to complete. Finding an example will not be easy for many. The paper itself will probably be quite short.

Limits and Popular Culture

John Greer

The basic concept of limits can be found in many facets of life. One such facet is art. The idea of limits, as a function approaches infinity, is especially common in many forms of art. I will be looking at one form of art, music. More specifically, I will be looking at the concept of limits and how it affects a song written by the popular Rock and Roll group, U2.

One type of limit, is the idea of the limit of a function as x approaches infinity. In this type of function, one could theoretically keep inputing an increasingly large or small number of x values for ever , yet the resulting y values will never reach the limit of that function. However, the resulting y values will get closer and closer to that limit. This idea of striving for a goal (or limit) that is impossible to reach, has a very disheartening effect and has been used time and time again by artists.

The group, U2, uses the basic idea of limits in their song, "I Still Haven't Found What I'm Looking For." The song begins by telling the story of somone who has travelled far and wide to search for somone, but has not been successful. The song talks about how this person has climbed mountains, run through fields, crawled and scaled walls only to reach this one person, but has not been successful. These lines give an artistic expression of the concept of limits. A

function will always be approaching its limit, but will not be succesful. For example, the function y=1/x has a limit of zero as x approaches infinity. No matter how large x becomes, y will never reach zero, yet it will keep getting closer.

The idea of limits has often been used in music, as well as many other forms of art. I have used the song, "I Still Haven't Found What I'm Looking For," as an example. I feel it gives a very human expression of the concept of limits.

I really like this example. The steady background beat adds to the impression of moving perpetually onward without reaching the goal, like moving out the x axis and the curve not reaching 0. Good explanation.

10

WRITING ASSIGNMENT 4

A Moving Experience

You have worked many examples of motion problems. Many of these problems involve the motion of a projectile. Try creating one of these problems. Don't just change the numbers from one of the book problems. Try to be more creative. Projectiles can be anything from rocks to pianos. They can be thrown, catapulted, launched, or in any other way sent into the air. Whatever you decide to use, ask questions such as "How high did it go?" "When will it reach the maximum height?" "When will it strike the ground?" "What was its speed upon impact?" In addition to asking the questions, provide a detailed solution to the problem.

TEACHER NOTES 4
A Moving Experience

This is a fairly short assignment. It offers a chance for students to be creative. They will have worked motion problems in their regular assignments and may also have done so in a physics class. Here they have the chance to create their own. One possibility is for students to solve each other's problems or to use the best of them on another form of assessment. In grading the problems, look for creative situations, wise use of calculus techniques, and interesting questions asked. The following example from a musical student exhibits some interesting twists to the typical problem and incorporates more than just the standard questions.

Lance Horne

Calculus p. 5

Nutty Notes

A catapult hurls a man playing a piano in common time at 240 beats per minute. His acceleration is -10 m/s/s; at one second, his velocity is 30 m/s, and at two seconds, he is 80 ~~feet~~ *meters* in the air. He starts on a 'c' ascending chromatically in modulo 12. How high off the ground was the catapult? What note will he be playing when he is at his highest? When he crashes?

I knew that acceleration is the derivative of velocity, which is the derivative of position. So, my three main equations are:

$$y = 1/2\ at^2 + v_0 t + x_0 \qquad dy/dt = at + v_0 \qquad d^2y/dt^2 = a$$

If a equals -10 m/s^2, then one can substitute when $t = 1$ s and the velocity $= 30$ m/s $= dy/dt$:

$$30 = -10(1) + v_0 \qquad v_0 = 40\ m/s$$

Back in the original equation, when $t = 2$ s , $y = 80$ ~~feet~~ *meters* and the height of the catapult is x_0:

$$80 = 1/2(-10)\ 2^2 + 40\ (2) + x_0 \qquad x_0 = 20\ meters\ above\ the\ ground$$

I then found the man's highest point and crashing point, (when $y' = 0$ and $y = 0$, respectively):

$$y' = -10t + 40 \quad 0 = -10t + 40 \quad t = 4\ seconds$$

$$y = 1/2\ (-10)t^2 + 40t + 20 \quad -20 = -5t^2 + 40t \qquad t = -.47,\ 8.47\ seconds\ (\ neg.\ not\ applicable)$$

So at the top of his parabola, 4 seconds have passed. 240 beats per minute $/60 = 4$ notes/sec. 16 notes have elapsed on this system:

16-12= 4, which is an E natural.

At crashing point, 8.47 seconds have elapsed. We can assume he is .03 seconds early hitting his next note, so 8.47 $\cong$ 8.5; at 4 notes per second, that is 34 notes minus 2(12)=10, which is a B^b, which he it hitting as he crashes.

excellent!

WRITING ASSIGNMENT 5

The Meaning of Mean

The Mean Value Theorem is one of the most important in the rigorous development of the calculus. Understanding it is important. To make it more understandable and relevant, write a paraphrase of this theorem. Do not use any mathematical terminology. Use only everyday language so that anyone who reads it will understand it. Be sure to include all of the conditions of the hypothesis in your paraphrase.

The Mean Value Theorem

If 1. f is differentiable for all values of x in the open interval (a, b), and

2. f' is continuous at $x = a$ and $x = b$,

then there is at least one number $x = c$ in (a, b) such that
$$f'(c) = \frac{f(b) - f(a)}{b - a}$$

TEACHER NOTES 5
The Meaning of Mean

This is a difficult assignment. While it is a short paper, it will not be easy to write. Students may not realize how much mathematical terminology they know until they try to write something without using any at all. Use your own discretion as to whether or not to allow such words as "curve," "line," "point," and "parallel." This is not an easy assignment, but one that will cause them to think seriously about the meanings of all the mathematical terms used daily in calculus. The continuous function can be modeled with a piece of cooked spaghetti, a snake, a worm, or a highway. All must be arranged so that they do not double back on themselves and have no sharp corners. This establishes what it is to be a function and to be differentiable. The slope of the tangent or secant between the endpoints can be demonstrated by a piece of uncooked spaghetti, a string pulled tight, or any other straight object.

Writing a paraphrase may be new to students. Here is a statement of the Sandwich Theorem and a paraphrase that you might want to share as an example.

$$\text{"Suppose that } f(x) \leq g(x) \leq h(x) \text{ for all } x \neq c \text{ in some interval}$$
$$\text{about } c \text{ and that } \lim_{x \to c} f(x) = \lim_{x \to c} h(x) = L. \text{ Then } \lim_{x \to c} g(x) = L.\text{"}$$

Have you ever looked at a map showing airline routes? I was looking at one the other day and noticed a flight from Fairbanks to Philadelphia with a stop in Chicago. I saw another flight from Honolulu to Orlando that also stops in Chicago. Of course, the Fairbanks to Philadelphia route was always north of the Honolulu to Orlando route. I saw a third flight that originated in Seattle and went to Atlanta. Unfortunately my map was a bit tattered, and I couldn't read all of it clearly. I could see, though, that the route from Seattle to Atlanta was always south of the route from Fairbanks to Philadelphia. I could also see that the route from Seattle to Atlanta stayed north of the route from Honolulu to Orlando. Knowing this, I figured out that the Seattle-to-Atlanta flight must also pass through Chicago.

Maggie Hulce
January 7, 1997
AP Calculus

THE MEANING OF MEAN

In order to understand the Mean Value Theorem imagine the following scenario which represents one of the numerous real life applications of this concept. One of the most basic examples of the usefulness of this theorem relates to motion. Imagine, for example, that you are looking at a picture which shows how far away from your hometown you were over the span of one hour while you were driving from your hometown towards California. Assuming that you are driving on the highway so you did not stop to use the restroom or to pick up McDonald's, or even at a stop sign for the entire hour, the picture would show that you were moving farther away from your hometown faster or slower as you were speeding up and slowing down with traffic (which should look like a picture of a wave). Now, put your finger somewhere on this picture that represents how far you were from your house sometime within the first 15 minutes of your trip. Do the same thing somewhere on the picture to represent how far you were sometime during the last 15 minutes of your trip. Now, remembering where you placed your fingers on the picture, take a ruler, or some type of straight-edged device and place it on the picture so that it hits both of these places. This theorem says that sometime after the first 15 minutes of the trip and before the last 15 minutes of the trip, your car was moving at a speed that the position of the ruler on the picture represents. To find when this happens take a pencil and line it up so it lies side by side with the ruler. Now, move the pencil (so that it still lines up with the tilt of the ruler) away from the ruler until it crosses a place in the picture where the pencil only touches one part of the wave. (This place will exist somewhere between the two places you originally placed your fingers.) Once the pencil reaches the place where it only touches one place, you have proved this theorem, which says that between any two places on this wave, if you put a ruler over both of them, there will be a place on the wave in between those other two places when how fast the car is moving is the same as how fast the car would have been moving if its path was straight along the ruler instead of in a wave.

Mark ....gr....

WRITING ASSIGNMENT 6

The Same, Yet Different

It has been said that calculus is the study of three things: derivatives, integrals, and integrals. The two types of integrals, definite and indefinite, are similar yet very different. Explain the similarities and differences between the two types of integrals. Then explain how the Fundamental Theorem of Calculus connects all three things: derivatives, integrals, and integrals. Do not just quote your textbook. Try to put these ideas into your own words.

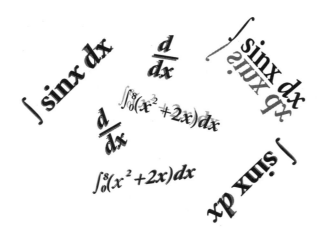

TEACHER NOTES 6
The Same, Yet Different

I believe that this is perhaps the most difficult writing assignment in this collection. It is a major assignment. It is easy for students to simply restate the Fundamental Theorem of Calculus. However, in this assignment you are looking for more than that. The differences between definite and indefinite integrals are very important. Indefinite integrals are families of functions. Definite integrals are distinct values or, if one of the limits is a variable, a specific function. The Fundamental Theorem connects the two by indicating that the specific value of a definite integral can be found through the functions defined by the indefinite integral. The definite integral is the limit of a Riemann sum. The indefinite integral is simply the undoing of differentiation. The beauty of the Fundamental Theorem is that the second of these can be used to find the first. Seemingly different concepts and starting points come together in one statement. Seeing this connection and being able to articulate it is difficult. This is an assignment that generally needs at least one rewrite before you can be sure that the student understands the concepts.

Calculus 5th hr
Jin-young yu

The same,
yet Different

- The relationship between definite and indefinite integrals-

There are two types of integrals;definite and indefinite. They are the same in the aspect of that they are the areas under the curve, however, they have differences.

Definite integrals are the areas under the curve in the given interval [a,b]. We write definite integral as:

$$\int_a^b f(x)\,dx.$$

We call [a,b] the **interval of integration**. The numbers are the **limits of integration**; a being the **lower limit of integration**, b being the **upper limit of integration**. We evaluate the definite integral by finding the value of $\int_a^b f(x)\,dx$ using **fnint** or **the fundamental theorem of calculus**. Thus, we can say the form $\int_a^b f(x)\,dx$ represents a number.

However, indefinite integral is an integral without any boundaries. we write as:

$$\int f(x)\,dx$$

Because one does not have the given interval, it is impossible to use a calculator(fnint) to evaluate the indefinite integral, so that one is encouraged to be aware of the fundamental theorem of calculus. The fundametal theorem of calculus connects these two types of integrals together. The second part of the fundamental theorem tells us that the definite integral of a continuous function from a to b can be found from any one of the function's antiderivatives F as the number $F(b) - F(a)$. And because antiderivatives make it possible to evaluate definite integrals by calculating numbers, therefore we can evaluate indefinite integrals by using antiderivatives of those functions and by adding a constant **C**, called **constant of integration** or **arbitrary constant**.

$$\int f(x)\,dx = F(x) + C$$

By fundamental theorem, every continuous function has an antiderivative. And that fact indicates that every continuous function has an indefinite integral. From this conclusion, we can relate an indefinite integral to a definite integral, as a definite integral of a function $f(x)$ being only a part(in the interval of integration)of indefinite integral of the same function. *Need more on the 1st part of the Fundamental Theorem.*

WRITING ASSIGNMENT 7

Heads or Tails, Disks or Shells

There are two methods for finding the volume of a solid of revolution: the disk/washer method and the shell method. How do you decide which method to use? Does it make a difference? Are there situations where one is better than the other? Create examples to demonstrate your reasoning.

A WATCHED CUP NEVER COOLS
© 1999 Key Curriculum Press

TEACHER NOTES 7
Heads or Tails, Disks or Shells

In this paper students must describe both of the basic methods for determining volumes of solids of revolution. In addition, they are asked to determine how to decide when to use each one. Look for an understanding of each method and the differences between them. The examples created should demonstrate students' points and not be trivial. This paper is an appropriate one to assign as a review and summary of this topic. Doing a thorough job of explaining these methods and their relative advantages will strengthen a student's understanding of the material. Look for proper use of vocabulary, clarity of explanation, and appropriate examples.

To find the volume of a solid that is defined by a function rotated around an axis an integral can be used. This essentially cuts the function into slices. These slices can be a number of things. Two of the most commonly used formats are the disk/washer method and the shell method. These are the approaches we use when looking at volumes that have a hole through the middle. The disk/washer method uses integration to stack up an infinite amount of infinitely small washers from top to bottom so to speak. The shell method uses hollow, concentric cylinders layered from the inside-out like an onion. In both of these methods the outside and inside are defined by a function or number of functions. The methods are very similar analytically with the exception of certain varying components, but the question arises which method do chose?

Determining whether to use the washer method or the shell method is fairly simple. Many times both methods can be used. The real question is when not to use one of the methods. If your washer or shell gets split up due to a curve in the function you probably no longer want to use that method. You could continue with your method but you would have to split it up into sections and the other method will probably fit the solid better.

Let's look at a few examples to see how these cylinders and washers can get split up. The equation $y=-x^2+2$ rotated around the y axis forms a paraboloid. The equation $y=x$ rotated around the y axis makes a cone. If the volume between the two surfaces has to

be found from $y=0$ to $y=1$ then an integral for the washer method or the shell method could be used.

washer method: $\pi r^2 h - \pi r_i^2 h = \pi \int_0^1 x^2 \, dy - \pi \int_0^1 x_i^2 \, dy$

($\pi r^2 h$ is the formula for the volume of a cylinder; washer is a cylinder with a cylinder shape missing in the middle. thus the idea that we can just subtract one equation from the other to get that hollow shape. The height for each washer/slice is infinitely small, thus dy is used.)

to find x we solve the equations for x
$y=-x^2+2 \qquad y=x$ (duh!)
$y_2=-x^2$
$x^2=-y+2$ so $\pi \int_0^1 (\sqrt{-y+2})^2 \, dy - \pi \int_0^1 y^2 \, dy$
$x=\sqrt{-y+2}$

$\pi \int_0^1 -y+2 \, dy - \pi \int_0^1 y^2 \, dy = -\frac{y^2}{2}+2y-\frac{y^3}{3} \Big]$

and so on

Using the shell method:

$2\pi \int r_1 h_1 - r_2 h_2 \, dx = 2\pi \int x(x) - x(-x^2+2) \, dx$

(Notice that we use dx here and dy above. We do this because the direction of our slices change. Since the shells are only lateral surfaces of cylinders with a minute thickness (dx) we don't need to subtract to get a hole in the middle. We can just use this method.)

That is a situation that works both ways. Sometimes one of these methods can't be used. For example: The volume between $y=-(x+5)^2+8$ and $y=-x+5$ from $x=2.6278$ to $x=8.3723$ when rotated around the y-axis. Here we can not use washers. At a certain height the washers are no longer bound by two equations, but by one

(from the dotted line up to the top of the parabola the washers bounds are defined by only one equation)

If we really wanted to use washers we could break everything into parts. It will be much easier to do the shell method. The shells are always (between our limits) defined by two equations and this will give us one nice integral

Certain times the shell method isn't always the best. Let's look at an example:

We see that if we want to use shells that they get spit up when $x=7$ to 10. The washer method will work much better the equations would just be $x=5$ and $x=\sqrt{9-y^2}+7$.

By thinking about how both of these methods work and looking at the graphs it is not incredibly difficult to tell which method to use. Solids of revolution are great!

WRITING ASSIGNMENT 8

The Game's Afoot

The following is a synopsis of the first part of an unpublished story. Your task is to solve the mystery and write the rest of the story. Your conclusion must include the mathematics of the solution. It should be written in story form and incorporate the mathematics within the dialogue and other prose as smoothly and naturally as possible. Be creative, but don't arrest the wrong individual!

The Case of the Cooling Corpse

It was a dark and stormy night. Holmes and Watson were called to the scene of the murder by Inspector Lestrade of the police. The victim was a wealthy but cruel man. He had many enemies.

The most likely suspects are the wife, the business partner, and the butler. Each has an equally strong motive. Each also has an alibi. The wife claims to have spent the entire evening at the theater across town. She was seen leaving the theater at 10:30 p.m. and returned home at 11:00 p.m., going straight up to her bedroom. Her return was verified by the upstairs maid. The business partner claims to have spent the evening working on papers at the office. His wife and household staff verified that he returned home at 10:30 p.m. The butler was on his night off. He claims to have been at the local pub until 10:00 p.m. The butler returned to his quarters above the carriage house at 10:05 p.m. and did not leave. This was verified by the other servants.

The body was found in the victim's study. Holmes arrived at the scene at 4:30 a.m. The room was unusually warm and stuffy. One of the police officers went to open a window. Holmes admonished him to delay that action until he had completed his investigation of the crime scene. He instructed Watson to determine the temperature of the body. This was found to be 88.0°. Holmes questioned the servants as to the room temperature during the evening and learned that the man had liked the room warm and that the temperature in the study was always very near the current 76°. Holmes asked Watson to take the temperature of the body again at the conclusion of his inspection of the scene, two hours after the first reading. It was 85.8°.

The Game's Afoot

This is a fun paper to write. The mathematics are relatively simple to compute and the mystery is not too difficult. Writing the story ending as a story, though, and incorporating the mathematics within the dialogue is a bit of a challenge. Students seem to enjoy doing it, though. Trying to explain how Holmes does logarithms and uses the number *e* without the aid of a calculator gives students a chance to be very creative. Look for smooth incorporation of mathematics, natural dialogue, and, of course, the correct solution to the mystery. By the way, the butler didn't do it. It was the business partner. Working out the time of death from Newton's law of cooling, Holmes discovers that the wealthy but cruel man was killed at 10:15 p.m. The only one without an alibi for the crucial time is the business partner.

20

The Game's Afoot
Parker Eberhard

Luckily for Inspector Lestrade, Holmes was a former math student of the famous Kamischke duo and he knew what was going on. As Watson continued to dust the area for fingerprints and look for DNA samples on the body, he noticed that Homes was sitting at the table with a pencil and paper and what seemed to be a small tele-communications center.

"This is no time to be surfing the net!" shouted Watson.

"I'm not," replied Holmes. "Anyways, I had my e-mail account taken away for sending a chain letter so there is no way that I could surf the net. I'm trying to solve a murder mystery."

"But how, Holmes?" Watson asked curiously.

"Well, while you are trying to search for clues all over the place, I am using the clues right my nose."

"I don't see anything under your nose but your mouth and your hot, smelly breath," Watson replied somewhat sarcastically.

"Exactly!!!" shouted Holmes; a wide grin appearing on his face.

"Uhhh, what are you talking about, I don't understand?"

"It's all very simple, Watson. See, using my TI CBL unit I can determine the temperature of the dead body; of which it is 85.8°F. I know that two hours ago the body's temperature was 88.0°F, and that the temperature of the room was kept at 76°F. Do you understand so far?"

Watson nodded his head and signaled for Holmes to proceed.

"Well, using one of the the many things that I learned in calculus, Newton's Law of Cooling ($T - T_s = (T_o - T_s)e^{-kt}$), I can determine the rate at which the body cooled and therefore determine the time at which the body started its cooling process; the time the murder was committed. We can substitute the 88.0°F for T_o and 76°F for T_s like so:

$$T - 76°F = (88.0°F - 76°F)e^{-kt}$$

We know that the body's temperature is 85.8°F right now at time 2 so we can plug this into the equation given us:

$$85.8°F - 76°F = (88.0°F - 76°F)e^{-k2}$$

With this equation, we can solve for K to find the rate at which the body cooled:

$$9.8°F = (12°F)e^{-k2}$$
$$9.8°F/12°F = e^{-k2}$$
$$.817 = e^{-k}$$

Do you still understand, Watson?"

"Kind of. But what is that e^{-k} stuff?"

"That has to do with natural logs and strange gardeners, but enough of that. You see, with this equation and some help from the calculator, I can find the rate at which the body cooled." After consulting his calculator, Holmes concluded that the rate of the cooling of the body was:

$$(\ln .817)/-2 = k$$
$$.10126 = k$$

"I can then plug this rate back into my equation along with 98.6°F and come up with the following:

$$88°F - 76°F = (98.6°F - 76°F)e^{-.10126t}$$
$$12°F/22.6°F = e^{-.10126t}$$
$$(\ln (.531))/-.10126 = t$$
$$6.25 = t$$

"This 6.25 is the number of hours that the body had cooled, Watson. Six hours and fifteen minutes before we took the first reading at 4:30am was when the murder occurred. Therefore, the murder occurred at 10:15pm and was preformed by the business man while he was in route from the office to his house."

"You're a genius Holmes, a genius. How on earth did you learn to do that?"

"Calculus, my Watson. Calculus."

WRITING ASSIGNMENT 9

Story Time

Write a story involving an exponential function built on this quote expressed by Jakob Bernoulli, a great Swiss mathematician: "Though changed, I shall arise the same." The quote may show up as a moral or punch line. The exponential function may take on a life of its own or something in the story may be growing or decaying exponentially. This is not an essay on exponential functions. It is a work of fiction. Be creative.

TEACHER NOTES 9
Story Time

This is another creative writing exercise. The quote from Jakob Bernoulli is on his gravestone. However, it can apply to the exponential function since under differentiation and integration it stays the same. The exponential function may show up as exponential growth in a population, the depth of snow, or as another physical object. Alternatively, the exponential function may be a metaphor of another process. In all cases, change occurs and the function, in whatever guise, remains the same. Two examples of student writing are included here to show the variety of stories possible.

20

Lin Wang
3rd hr

Story Time

At the time of her caretaker's death, she gave no thought to his whispered words, "Though changed, I shall arise the same." What seemed more important was her grief. Automatically, from years of proper teaching, she went through the appropriate motions of mourner. She was donned in the Institution approved white. Her hair had been tied back and her skin sterilized. The androgynous smock worn by all prepubescents, as always, chafed uncomfortably against her. It was deemed unfair by her that she had to portray a veneer of impassivity while all she wanted to do was anything but that. It was not the first time she disagreed with Institution rules and also not the first time that she did nothing about it. While the funeral proceedings took place, she was struck by a myth whispered conspiratorially one stagnant night.

"The Firebird," her caretaker whispered, "was a most glorious creature." The child crowded around his feet. Tales were rare and forbidden tales even more so. "She was hatched from an egg so white and so pure. She arose mewling and blind like all chicks but with an intensity of emotion unequaled in the Bird Kingdom."

"Why was she called the firebird?" she asked, as all children do.

"Because, honey-child, she was a fiery little thing. Instead of feathers, she wore tiny flames as raiment. And as she grew, her flames flickered even more fiercely, and her powers grew great. Growth, dearest, was fast when she was young but as she reached her prime, she grew no more."

"What happened to her?"

"Why, honey-child, many adventures. But the night is getting on, and your bed calls out to you."

And now the caretaker would never again be able to spin any stories. There would be no more delirious tales of giant sea serpents or of feminine great eyes unleashing vast powers. Most of all, there would be no more tales of the Firebird, whose beginnings she heard long ago and whose future she never heard. She glanced around to see if anyone was watching her. When she deemed it to be safe, she opened the package her caretaker pressed into her hand right before he was taken away. Oh, such beauty! A miniature bird hung from delicate chains. Though wrought from gold,

---

it seemed to beam an inferno of its own. The Firebird's fate grabbed brutally at her curiosity, and she waited impatiently for the funeral's end.

She dug furiously through the pile of books her caretaker deeded to her. Her mother had been infuriated by The Book of Myth since it was illegal to own fiction privately, but her caretaker hid it carefully in the bindings of a quite safe and legal book. Ah, there it was. After checking once again to see if the door was locked, she settled lotus position on the ground. "Ew," she crinkled her nose at the title, "The Book of Exponentials." She turned the cover and gazed at confusion at the graphs and math symbols. She continued flipping. She had often seen the caretaker seated at the edge of her bed with the book in hand. What he read weren't graphs or symbols but myths. All she saw here weren't myths or tales. She turned a few more pages in frustration. On the edge of a page, she saw something written in a neat, precise fashion. She rotated the book and read,

note: exponential functions reflect life. as children growth progresses rapidly but growth slows and eventually reaches a stopping point. and then death.

Curious, she thought. She flipped a few more pages until she came upon another note:

note: is immortality possible? refer to the Phoenix.

The Phoenix? She turned to the middle of the book. Ah, there was his secret. The Book of Myths lay between the sheets of The Book of Exponentials. She turned to the index and sought out a tale of the Phoenix. She turned to it and read, "The Phoenix, or the Firebird, originated from a large white egg." The Phoenix and the Firebird were one and the same, she thought excitedly. She skimmed to the end, "At the time of the Phoenix' death, she was consumed by a large and unforgiving fire. However, the ashes after the pyre died down cradled another Firebird egg. And thus the cycle of immortality continues."

It ended with a quote from Jakob Bernoulli, an ancient Swiss mathematician, "Though changed, I shall arise the same."

She unconsciously swung the chain in her hand, and the Firebird flew back and forth with every swing. The words of the caretaker reverberated in her mind, but still she didn't understand its meaning. However, with youth comes impatience. She stored the day's learnings for another day.

excellent story. I would like to read more of this child's adventures.

WRITING ASSIGNMENT 10

Why Do We Have to Learn This?

Why should you learn the techniques of integration, such as integration by parts, trigonometric substitution, and partial fractions? Computers and even some graphing calculators can do integration analytically much more quickly than you will ever be able to do so by hand. Should these techniques be dropped from the course completely? What emphasis do you feel should be placed on pencil and paper integration in general? Just how much is necessary or beneficial to learn of these skills? Justify your answer.

$$\int \ln \left(\sqrt{x} + \sqrt{1 + x}\right) dx$$

$$\int \frac{\cos x \, dx}{\sqrt{4 - \cos^2 x}}$$

TEACHER NOTES 10
Why Do We Have to Learn This?

This is a question students often ask. When studying the more complex techniques of integration, it is a real issue. In fact it is a question that many teachers ask themselves when dealing with these topics. Certainly it is easier to use a symbolic manipulator on either a calculator or a computer. Is there any value in learning to perform these manipulations by hand? And just how much of this should we teach and then expect our students to be able to do? When I first assigned this question I did not know what to expect as answers from my students. Their responses have helped me to shape my own teaching of these topics and to put these techniques in perspective. Learning complex techniques of integration helps students to put together many of the ideas previously learned. It teaches them to analyze and think about problems. These are valuable skills. Whether or not they remember how to do trigonometric substitution in six months is not as important to me as that they know how to look at any complex problem, mathematical or otherwise, and break it down into manageable parts. This paper can be quite lengthy as students search for the answers to these questions both in discussion with others and internal reflection.

WRITING ASSIGNMENT *11*

What Was It All About Anyway?

Now that you are approaching the end of the course, consider all you have learned. Just exactly what is calculus anyway? Be complete and yet concise in your answer.

TEACHER NOTES 11
What Was It All About Anyway?

This is typically an end-of-the-course question. It is a major assignment. This paper is a chance for students to reflect back on their year and figure out exactly what they were learning. What does calculus mean to them, anyway? Answers can take one of two forms. Some students will give a very mathematical definition of the two branches of calculus and their applications. Others will give a more personal reflection on what it meant to them. Both are acceptable answers. Look for clarity of thought and presentation along with correct mathematical understanding. This paper could also be given partway through the course to assess students' understanding at that point.

20

Naomi Beeman
hr. 5
"what is calculus?" essay
    As our book says in the introduction to chapter five, calculus is the most important application of mathematics in the world. Other branches of mathematics, such as geometry, teach us how to find the area and volume of shapes that are made out of straight lines or perfect circles, but the majority of things in the real world are not made out of straight lines and circles. Many things in the real world are very irregular. They are oddly shaped. They are wavy and bumpy. Calculus can be used to find the area or volume of these "real-world" objects.
    The methods employed in calculus to determine the volume and area of odd shapes are actually not very unlike those used in a geometry class. In geometry, we learned simple equations to find the area and volume of shapes made from circles and straight lines. In calculus we learn how to divide strange shapes into an infinite number of infinitely thin circles, trapezoids or rectangles, which are familiar shapes whose areas we do know how to find. We then manipulate our function by using definite integrals to add the areas of the infinite number of infinitely thin shapes together to get the total area or volume of the stange shape. The simple equations from geometry are combined with the new concepts of integration to form a process of finding areas and volumes that is, unlike geometry, applicable to almost any shape you could ever think of.
    Calculus has many applications besides finding the area or volume of strangely shaped objects. Calculus is about change. We can use calculus to describe the rate at which a population grows, an object falls, or a reservoir empties. We find rates of change not through the use of integrals, but with derivatives. If we have an equation for the position of an object or the number of

individuals in a population or the volume in a reservoir through time, and we take the derivative of that function, we will get an equation that describes the rate at which the population or volume or position changes over time. A derivative gives us the slope of the function's tangent line at any given point. In algebra, we learned to find the slope of a straight line. If our original equation was a linear one, then there would be no need for calculus. The rate of change would remain the same forever. However, when dealing with real world situations, this is not very often going to be the case. Think about populations. Do they keep on growing forever? No. Population is dependant upon what the environment can support. You might also think about moving objects. They usually don't keep going forever. A car drives at different speeds depending on what type of street it's on. It also slows to a stop before stop signs and red lights. Calculus allows us to interpret the movement of objects whose describing equations are not linear, but factor in things such as limitations on population growth and variable velocity.

Section five point four of our book, which introduces the fundamental theorem of calculus, spews some mumbo jumbo about presenting the discovery by Newton and Leibniz of the "astonishing connections between integration and differentiation." To me, the astonishing thing about calculus is not the connection between integration and differentiation, but the brilliant way that it combines the simple methods of algebra and geometry with the important discovery of Newton and Leibniz to form a math with more real-world applications than any other before or since. Calculus is the study of the real world. Calculus can be used to do everything from finding lengths, areas, volumes, and average values of functions, to predicting future population sizes and costs of living, to describing planetary motion, buisness cycles, and brain

waves. Calculus is a beautiful combination the obvious and the brilliant that allows people in almost every field of study to describe our world, irregular and imperfect as it is.

SAMPLE LAB ACTIVITY REPORT

PURPOSE

The purpose of this lab is to observe the behavior of a bouncing basketball in terms of height over time. Using numerical values of the points representing the position of the basketball in relation to the CBL, we are to model the velocity of the basketball using the idea of finite differences. After this is done, we are to use derivatives to find the average velocity of the bouncing basketball. After we have found the average velocity of our system, we are to once again use the idea of derivatives to fing the acceleration of the ball as it bounces.

Once we have determined the average velocity and the acceleration of the bouncing system on the earth, we are to find the average velocity and the acceleration of the same bouncing basketball, but on a planet with a gravitational acceleration other than that of earth. We choose the planet Saturn, which has a gravitational acceleration of 9.1 m/s.^{2}.

What Goes Up, Must Come Down

Parker Eberhard
Stephanie Teply
Freddy Yarur

10/23/96

PART I: COLLECTING DATA

The purpose of this part of the lab is to collect the data necessary to generate a graph of the position of a ball as it bounces many times. In order to do this, we ran a sonic probe device, which was positioned approximately two meters off of the ground, through the CBL unit to our calculator. We then selected the program 'DROP' from the various programs in our calculator and prepared it for data collection. When everything was ready, we held the basket ball one-half meter below the probe and ran the program. Once we heard the clicking from the sonic probe, we released the ball and let it bounce until the program was finished running. We ran the experiment four more times so we could use the most accurate data we could attain.

The data that we collected was displayed in a graph like the following:

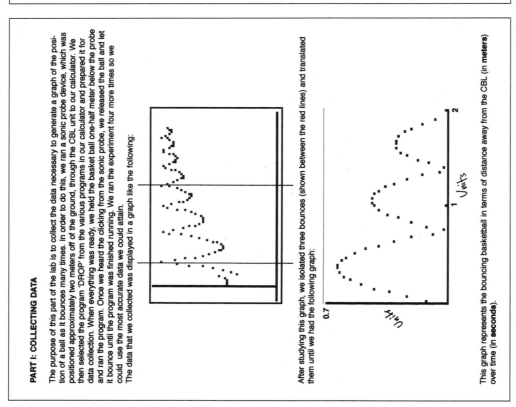

After studying this graph, we isolated three bounces (shown between the red lines) and translated them until we had the following graph:

This graph represents the bouncing basketball in terms of distance away from the CBL (in **meters**) over time (in **seconds**).

ACTUAL VALUES OF POINTS ON GRAPH OF TIME vs. DISTANCE	
TIME (sec) (x)	DISTANCE (meters from ground) (y)
0.00	0.00000
0.04	0.13281
0.08	0.24805
0.12	0.35342
0.16	0.44342
0.20	0.51696
0.24	0.57513
0.28	0.61904
0.32	0.64648
0.36	0.65745
0.40	0.65526
0.44	0.63879
0.48	0.60587
0.52	0.55538
0.56	0.48952
0.60	0.41269
0.64	0.32159
0.68	0.21183
0.72	0.08671
0.76	0.01975
0.80	0.12732
0.84	0.22061
0.88	0.29744
0.92	0.36000
0.96	0.40610
1.00	0.43903
1.04	0.45330
1.08	0.45550
1.12	0.44232
1.16	0.41488
1.20	0.37098
1.24	0.31720
1.28	0.24476
1.32	0.15476
1.36	0.05158
1.40	0.01975
1.44	0.10756
1.48	0.18000
1.52	0.23708
1.56	0.27878
1.60	0.30403
1.64	0.31281
1.68	0.31061
1.72	0.29305
1.76	0.26122
1.80	0.21732
1.84	0.15476
1.88	0.07683

TIME (sec) (x)	DISTANCE (meters from ground) (y)	SLOPE (DERIVATIVE)
0.00	0.00000	3.3206
0.04	0.13281	2.8808
0.08	0.24805	2.6340
0.12	0.35342	2.2501
0.16	0.44342	1.8383
0.20	0.51696	1.4542
0.24	0.57513	1.0976
0.28	0.61904	0.6860
0.32	0.64648	0.2744
0.36	0.65745	-0.0548
0.40	0.66526	-0.4117
0.44	0.63879	-0.8232
0.48	0.60587	-1.2630
0.52	0.55538	-1.6460
0.56	0.48952	-1.9210
0.60	0.41269	-2.2780
0.64	0.32159	-2.7440
0.68	0.21183	-3.1290
0.72	0.08671	UNDEFINED ?
0.76	0.01975	2.6893
0.80	0.12732	2.3323
0.84	0.22061	1.9208
0.88	0.29744	1.5645
0.92	0.36000	1.1525
0.96	0.40610	0.8234
1.00	0.43903	0.3567
1.04	0.45330	0.0549
1.08	0.45550	-0.3293
1.12	0.44232	-0.6860
1.16	0.41488	-1.0980
1.20	0.37098	-1.3450
1.24	0.31720	-1.8110
1.28	0.24476	-2.2500
1.32	0.15476	-2.2580
1.36	0.05158	UNDEFINED ?
1.40	0.01975	2.1958
1.44	0.10756	1.8110
1.48	0.18000	1.4270
1.52	0.23708	1.0426
1.56	0.27878	0.6311
1.60	0.30403	0.2195
1.64	0.31281	-0.0549
1.68	0.31061	-0.4391
1.72	0.29305	-0.7958
1.76	0.26122	-1.0980
1.80	0.21732	-1.5640
1.84	0.15476	-1.9480
1.88	0.07683	-2.2780

PART TWO: DETERMINING VELOCITY

The purpose of this part of the lab is to determine the velocity of the bouncing basketball using the derivatives of the lines created when we connect consecutive points on the graph of the distance-time data we have generated.

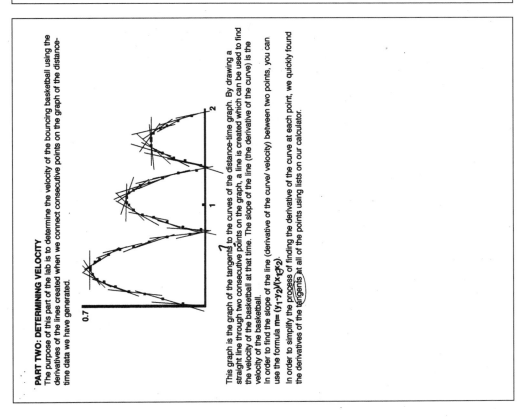

This graph is the graph of the tangents to the curves of the distance-time graph. By drawing a straight line through two consecutive points on the graph, a line is created which can be used to find the velocity of the basketball at that time. The slope of the line (the derivative of the curve) is the velocity of the basketball.

In order to find the slope of the line (derivative of the curve/ velocity) between two points, you can use the formula $m = (y_1 - y_2)/(x_1 - x_2)$.

In order to simplify the process of finding the derivative of the curve at each point, we quickly found the derivatives of the tangents at all of the points using lists on our calculator.

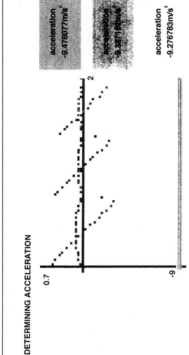

DETERMINING ACCELERATION

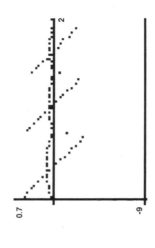

acceleration
-9.478077m/s²

acceleration
-9.3877 m/s²

acceleration
-9.276783m/s²

Once you have found the graph of the velocity of the basketball, you can find the acceleration of the basketball. In order to do this, you need to find the derivative of the line representing the velocity of the ball. Assuming that the graph of the velocity was linear, we only need to find an equation to fit this line. The slope of the line, representing the velocity is the derivative of that line as well as the numerical value of the acceleration of the basketball as it bounces. The graph of the slope of the acceleration will be a horizontal line due to the fact that the acceleration remains constant. Because we have three different curves with three different velocities, we had to find three different accelerations for the basketball. However, these accelerations are numerically very close to each other so it can be assumed that the acceleration is constant through the whole system.

This graph, the graph of the average acceleration of the bouncing basketball, shows the acceleration as being represented by a horizontal line at y=-9.380674. Therefore, the acceleration of the basketball is -9.380674m/s². According to the laws of the universe, this value for acceleration that we should have found is -9.8m/s², which is the value of the acceleration do to gravity on the surface of earth. Assuming that everything were perfect, we would have ended up with this value for

---

This graph is a graph of the velocity of the ball as well as the position of the ball during its bounces. The parabolic curves show the position of the ball and the diagonal lines show the velocity of the ball as it bounces. The diagonal lines showing the velocity of the ball were created by plotting the values of the slope of the tangent (the derivative) against the respective time.

Defined as the speed and direction of an object, velocity can clearly be seen on this graph. With the addition of the green line, it can be seen that when the ball is traveling in an upward motion towards the CBL unit, the velocity is positive. All derivatives taken for points representing the ball moving in an upward direction will have a positive slope. As the ball reaches its maximum height, represented by the green lines, the velocity becomes zero. The reason that the velocity is zero at this point is because the ball stops all motion for a split second at this point. If a tangent line were drawn to the curve at this point, the line would be horizontal and have a slope of zero. Because the slope of the tangent equals the velocity at that point, the velocity is zero. After reaching this point of no velocity, the ball starts its journey back towards the earth. Traveling away from the CBL unit, the ball has a negative velocity. This is shown on the graph by the line representing velocity being in the negative y values as the graph on the displacement of the ball curves back towards zero.

According to the graph, there is no velocity when the ball hits the ground. The reason for this can be explained both physically and mathematically. Using some of the ideas behind physics, you can conclude that the ball never stops moving when it hits the ground; it only changes directions. No matter how close you can get to the moment that the ball changes direction, you will never see the ball stop. It is therefore assumed that the ball never stops moving, it only changes velocity. Using some of the things that we know about lines and the slopes of lines, we can say that at the point when the ball hits the ground and changes direction, the velocity is undefined. If we were to draw lines tangent to the curve at the point where the ball hits the ground, we would find these lines to be vertical lines. Knowing that vertical lines have an undefined slope, it can be concluded that the velocity at this point in the ball's motion is undefined. The velocity at this point can be thought to be asymptotic and approaching infinity or negative infinity, depending on if the ball is approaching the ground or leaving the ground. The asymptotes in this system are represented by the magenta lines.

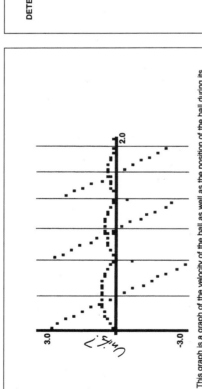

LAB ON SATURN WHERE GRAVITATIONAL ACCELERATION IS 9.1m/s^2

Because we only know calculus through derivatives, we could not use integrals to do derivatives backwards. Therefore, we had to devise our own method for finding the necessary data for creating an acceleration, velocity, and distance-time graph for the system if the lab were run on Saturn.

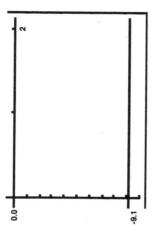

The above graph shows the constant acceleration on Saturn, which is also known as the gravitational pull. Assuming that time remains constant throughout our wonderful universe, the universe in which 47 is the most common number, we know that our x-values for the graph will be the same as those for the previous graphs. However, the height values will be slightly smaller, as the acceleration is 9.1 m/s^2 compared to earth's acceleration of 9.8 m/s^2. We take the original height values from the original three bounces used and multiply these heights by the ratio of 9.1(Saturn) /9.8 (Earth). This ratio is approx. .9285714, which means that Saturn's gravity is 92.86 % of earth's gravitational pull. Therefore, at the same time values, our height values are 96.86% smaller.

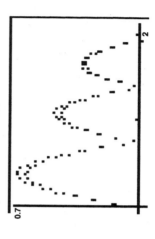

As we know that the height positions are .9286 of the original heights, we again use the methodology of finite differences described in the original part of the lab in order to find the derivatives. We

---

our acceleration. Unfortunately, not everything is perfect. With only a 4.28% percentage error, we weren't that terribly inaccurate, but we weren't accurate either. There are many things that factor into our acceleration being off from the actual acceleration; both mechanical and human. The thing that probably contaminated our data the most was the size of the basketball. Being as big as it was, the basketball could have moved around a lot, yet stayed in the path of the CBL's sonar beam. If the ball were to move, the sonar would hit areas on the ball which were either closer or farther away than the other areas where the sonar hit, giving us false distances. Another thing that could have lead to our incorrect value for gravitational acceleration is air resistance. Because the basketball was much larger than the Christmas tree bouncy ball, the air resistance on the basketball was much greater. If the experiment were done in a vacuum, the data may have been more accurate, provided us with a better value for gravitational acceleration. Another possibility was that the batteries on Freddy's calculator were dying. Besides these possibilities, we could have miscalculated some of the data. The tolerance of the calculator may also have some role in our incorrect answer.

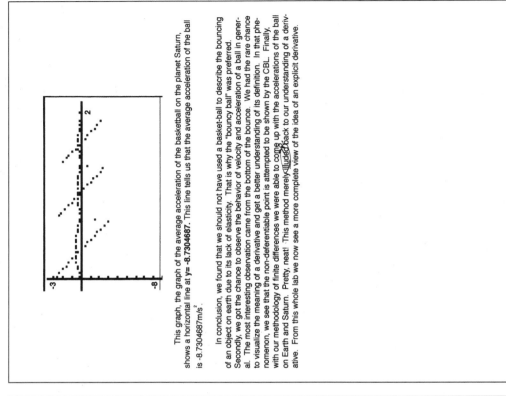

This graph, the graph of the average acceleration of the basketball on the planet Saturn, shows a horizontal line at y=-8.7304687. This line tells us that the average acceleration of the ball is -8.7304687m/s².

In conclusion, we found that we should not have used a basket-ball to describe the bouncing of an object on earth due to its lack of elasticity. That is why the "bouncy ball" was preferred. Secondly, we got the chance to observe the behavior of velocity and acceleration of a ball in general. The most interesting observation came from the bottom of the bounce. We had the rare chance to visualize the meaning of a derivative and get a better understanding of its definition. In that phenomenon, we see that the non-deferentiable point is attempted to be shown by the CBL. Finally, with our methodology of finite differences we were able to come up with the accelerations of the ball on Earth and Saturn. Pretty, neat! This method merely alluded back to our understanding of a derivative. From this whole lab we now see a more complete view of the idea of an explicit derivative.

then generate these derivative values, which are models of the velocity for the three values.

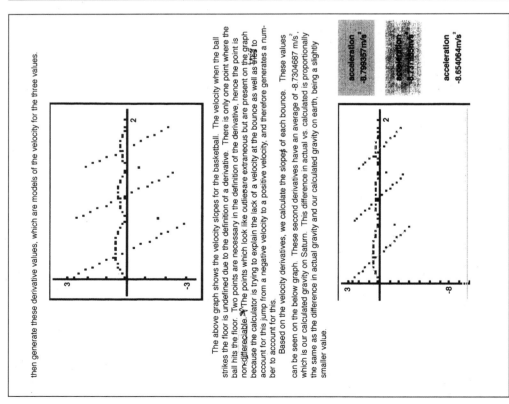

acceleration -8.799357m/s²

acceleration -6.??????m/s²

acceleration -8.654064m/s²

The above graph shows the velocity slopes for the basketball. The velocity when the ball strikes the floor is undefined due to the definition of a derivative. There is only one point where the ball hits the floor. Two points are necessary in the definition of the derivative, hence the point is non-differeciable. The points which look like outliers are extraneous but are present on the graph because the calculator is trying to explain the lack of a velocity at the bounce as well as trying to account for this jump from a negative velocity to a positive velocity, and therefore generates a number to account for this.

Based on the velocity derivatives, we calculate the slopes of each bounce. These values can be seen on the below graph. These second derivatives have an average of -8.7304687 m/s², which is our calculated gravity on Saturn. This difference in actual vs. calculated is proportionally the same as the difference in actual gravity and our calculated gravity on earth, being a slightly smaller value.